Light

of the

Word

HOW KNOWING

THE HISTORY OF THE BIBLE

ILLUMINATES OUR FAITH

SUSAN C. LIM

An imprint of InterVarsity Press
Downers Grove, Illinois

InterVarsity Press
P.O. Box 1400 | Downers Grove, IL 60515-1426
ivpress.com | email@ivpress.com

InterVarsity Press® is the publishing division of InterVarsity Christian Fellowship/USA®. For more information, visit intervarsity.org.

All Scripture quotations, unless otherwise indicated, are taken from The Holy Bible, New International Version®, NIV®. Copyright © 1973, 1978, 1984, 2011 by Biblica, Inc.™ Used by permission of Zondervan. All rights reserved worldwide. www.zondervan.com. The "NIV" and "New International Version" are trademarks registered in the United States Patent and Trademark Office by Biblica, Inc.™

While any stories in this book are true, some names and identifying information may have been changed to protect the privacy of individuals.

"Build on rock" photo by Susan C. Lim

The publisher cannot verify the accuracy or functionality of website URLs used in this book beyond the date of publication.

Cover design: David Fassett
Interior design: Jeanna Wiggins
Cover images: Getty Images: © Sebastian Condrea, © ajma_pl, © serge-75, © Philippe Lissac / GODONG
     manuscript of the New Testament from the 4th century / uncial 0169 (Gregory-Aland),
     Wikimedia Commons

ISBN 978-1-5140-0694-8 (print) | ISBN 978-1-5140-0695-5 (digital)

Printed in the United States of America ♾

Library of Congress Cataloging-in-Publication Data
A catalog record for this book is available from the Library of Congress.

30   29   28   27   26   25   24   23 | 13   12   11   10   9   8   7   6   5   4   3   2   1

DEDICATED TO BRIAN,

LIGHT BEARER

Contents

Introduction

LOVING GOD'S WORD

OUT OF GOD'S MANY GOOD GIFTS, salvation is primary. There is another gift, however, that's a close second: the gift of believing the Scriptures. Without the first, we cannot *know* God and be with him forever. Without the second, we cannot *experience* God as we should in the here and now.

Sometimes these gifts are given at once or in close succession. But for others, like me, there is a significant gap in time. I accepted Jesus as my Lord and Savior when I was a teenager, but then it took me over fifteen years to accept the Scriptures as God's Word. These first and second gifts are not automatically linked, and many Christians are unaware of this disconnect. My deepest prayer is that this book will help bridge this divide and cultivate our love and reverence for Jesus, who is both the Son of God and the Word of God.

Love is at the core of both gifts. Salvation means we receive God's love and love him in return; the same is true of the Scriptures. The second gift becomes our own when we read God's covenant of love to us and then wholeheartedly believe in and love the Word of God.

1

I fell in love with the Bible through an unexpected means: history. My historical research of the Scriptures blew my mind as I discovered how the dates, locations, and people in the Bible lined up with historical data. I marveled at ancient literature and archaeological finds that corroborated the Old and New Testament stories. The impact of these discoveries on my heart was equally seismic. My heart bowed in worship over and over as knowledge metabolized into faith and God's Word became living and active in me.

My discoveries, both academic and personal, are recorded in this book. I hope these facts and stories provide light for your spiritual journey.

FROM DARKNESS TO LIGHT

Darkness covered most of my childhood—the kind of darkness that leaves you scared and disoriented. Abuse, loneliness, and neglect were familiar companions, and I often cried myself to sleep. One night when I was twelve years old, I was drowning in tears, when out of nowhere a strange peace entered into the room. A transcendent love unlike anything I'd ever known wrapped around my soul. This feeling was more than a feeling. It was pure love. It was pure light. And I knew somehow at that moment that God was real.

My parents were Buddhists so my childhood understanding of God was tethered to their faith. We went to temple on weekends when my parents had time. The monk was warm and inviting, and he kindly answered all of my questions about life and spirituality. He even taught me some chants and rituals. But the more I learned about the Buddhist ways, I was certain that the God whom I had experienced was way bigger than anything that the monk described.

Despite this incredible experience of love and light, my day-to-day changed little. As I got older, I searched for acceptance in all the wrong places and found myself in more trouble and heartbreak than imaginable. Then one day, a friend invited me to join her high school youth group at a Presbyterian church. I disobeyed my parents and attended secretly, disregarding the ominous warning that the Christian "spirits," as my mom termed it, would bring bad luck to our Buddhist family. Little did I know then that the Christian "Spirit"—the Holy Spirit—would do more than any of us could have imagined.

I look back to that fateful night and the decades since, and I can mark two distinct moments when the Holy Spirit forever changed my course. The first was the moment of salvation. This was when the Holy Spirit opened my spiritual eyes and heart to wholeheartedly accept Jesus Christ as my Lord and Savior. Fifteen years later, the Holy Spirit led me to a second pivotal moment where I wholeheartedly accepted the entire Bible as the very words of the living God.

The first moment is what Christians throughout church history have sometimes called "the great confession" or "the good confession." In Matthew 16:15-16, Jesus asks his disciples, "Who do you say I am?" And Peter responds with the great confession: "You are the Messiah, the Son of the living God." Also, 1 John 4:13-15 states that those who abide in God have confessed that Jesus is "the Son of God" and "the Savior of the world." Likewise, the apostle Paul states in Romans 10:9, "If you declare with your mouth, 'Jesus is Lord,' . . . you will be saved." These all refer to the same good and great confession that Christians make when we come to believe that Jesus is Lord. That's what I call the "first confession."

But someone can believe that Jesus is Lord without understanding that the entire Bible is the Word of God. Even though I was a Christian, it took me years to fully accept Scripture for what it claims to be: God-breathed (2 Timothy 3:16) and the Word of God (John 1:1). To do so is also a miraculous working of the Holy Spirit. So when my heart and mind accepted the truth and authority of the Bible, it was a second transformative moment in my Christian life. I call this moment my "second confession," because it is almost as important as the first. First we confess "Jesus is Lord," and second we also confess "The Bible is the Word of God."

MY FIRST CONFESSION

I made my first confession during the spring of my senior year in high school. I was desperate for love and desperate for peace, and a friend had told me that there is a God, whose name is Jesus, who could provide both. It sounded too good to be true, and I wondered if this was a cult or some money-making scam. But my friend seemed genuine, so I followed her to church on a Friday night to attend a youth rally. The songs, the raising of hands, and the emotions all intrigued and, to some extent, worried me. Were these people delusional or making it up? Regardless, I stayed, observing the preacher, who spoke with passion about Jesus who can heal broken hearts and make all things new. My heart was shattered when I was seventeen, leaving me feeling irreparably broken and discarded. So I listened closely, hanging on to every word about this Jesus, who through his death and resurrection, offers new life in exchange for marred ones. These were the very words I needed to hear, but how could these promises be true?

After the sermon, small groups met to discuss the content and raise questions. I sat silently for most of the small-group session, but toward the end, the leader asked, "Who would like to invite Jesus into their hearts?" At that moment, God whispered into my heart, "That was me. And my name is Jesus." I knew implicitly that Jesus was referring to that encounter with light and love when I was twelve years old, and I believed everything that was shared about Christ that night. In that moment, the Holy Spirit convicted me of these eternal truths: I am a sinner. I needed a Savior. Jesus provided himself as the perfect sacrifice for all my sins. He resurrected from the dead. He claimed victory over death. And he calls me his own.

I cried rivers of tears that night, as if the years of abuse and sadness would be washed away in that torrent. And Jesus has indeed given me a new and resurrected life.

That night, however, no one told me that Jesus, who was now my Lord and Savior, was the fulfillment of prophecy or that there are four Gospel accounts to convey his truths. I was also unaware that there are sixty-six books in the entire Bible, thirty-nine in the Old Testament and twenty-seven in the New Testament. No one told me about the Council of Nicaea in AD 325, the Arian controversy, or the role of the church fathers regarding the compilation of the Bible. Did I need to know these facts to make the first confession? Absolutely not. My salvation was sealed that evening when I accepted Jesus as my Lord and Savior.

Perhaps your experience of salvation was similar. The experience and power of the Holy Spirit were more real than anything tangible. Like me, you might have made the first confession without a solid understanding of the Scriptures. You're not alone. That was my story and the story of countless others. A nuanced knowledge of the Scriptures is not a prerequisite for salvation.

The first and second confessions, however, are inextricably linked because Jesus, who is Lord and Savior, is also the Word of God. The God of our salvation is the God of the Scriptures. Jesus built his ministry on the Scriptures, and we believe in his death and resurrection as told in the Scriptures. God, in his divine wisdom and kind grace, has made himself accessible to humankind by donning human flesh and by revealing himself through words penned by humans.

Yet those who believe in the incarnation and resurrection of Christ might not know that the sixty-six books of the Bible are the true Word of God. In pews across the world, many genuine followers of Jesus do not believe that the entire Bible is the Word of God. The catch, however, is that many are unaware of this unbelief.

MY SECOND CONFESSION

Our first confession is typically accompanied by baptism and celebration. But our second confession largely goes unexamined. For me, the first and second confessions were not automatically linked. More importantly, I was unaware of their disconnect.

I spent over fifteen years as a Christian quoting, memorizing, studying, and teaching Scripture. At one point, I even wrote out the entire Bible by hand. But deep in my heart was an unbelief that festered without my knowing, and my unbeknownst secret came to light one random morning in 2007.

I was reading the Bible when the Holy Spirit stirred my soul and made me pause at the familiar verses. The Spirit convicted me of my unbelief in a gentle but firm manner by whispering into my spirit: "You don't believe what you're reading."

I remember saying out loud in response, "You're right . . . these words sound nice, but I don't believe that they're from you. How can they be? Written by men on parchment, handed down from generation to generation. And some of the stories in here . . . I just can't."

These words, this confession, tumbled out, and I hadn't even realized that they had taken residence in my soul. Had it not been the conviction of the Spirit, I would have vehemently denied my heresy! But here I was, telling God that the Bible was a sham.

The journey from that fateful morning in 2007 to now is a roadmap of sorts for this book. Your journey might look different, but I hope the lessons I've learned can clarify mysteries that shroud our understanding of God's Word. I'm a skeptic—that's just how I'm wired, and maybe that's how you tick. If that's the case, this book is for you. Christians are asked to base their entire lives on the Bible, but so few of us know how it was formed or what it declares.

Before someone buys a house or enters employment, the contract should be reviewed thoroughly. Christians are asked to trust in the Scriptures, yet many haven't read God's covenant in full before professing faith. While a comprehensive understanding of the Scriptures is not a prerequisite for salvation, it is nonnegotiable for sanctification.

Spiritual confusion and the high rate of deconversion, among other issues in the church, can be traced back to a lack of love and reverence for the Scriptures. Prior to my second confession, I failed to love or truly believe in the entire Bible. There were certain parts—such as the Gospels and the Psalms—that seemed more believable. But there were many (many) parts I did not believe or understand. I felt spiritually anemic, hoping that the next day would be better if I tried harder. I felt like I was groping in darkness and lost in my faith. But learning about the history of the Bible was like light dawning after a long and confusing season. So I share this light with all those who need encouragement in their faith journey.

HISTORICAL EVIDENCE

I've had the joy of teaching American history for over two decades. I fell in love with history as an undergraduate because understanding the past allows me to see the world today more clearly. I believe that's true for all of us.

Several years ago, JD, my son who was seven at the time, asked me, "Mom, why are there so many Spanish-speaking people in California but not in Canada?" We live in Southern California and had recently visited Canada, so the question was befitting. I told him about the history of North America, trying to keep it brief. JD loves history, though, so we talked about Indigenous Americans, European colonization, Spanish missions, the Treaty of Guadalupe Hidalgo, the Alamo, and the annexation of Texas.

His seven-year-old world became a lot more understandable because of historical context. It also taught him that the present cannot be divorced from the past. We can ignore the past intellectually, but we can never ignore it experientially. Not knowing the past easily leads to present-day confusion.

The same is true of knowing the history of the Bible. Knowing how God wove his Word through the ages serves as a light in our faith journey and rekindles our commitment to learning and living out the Scriptures. These chapters weave together primary sources, historical evidence, pivotal moments in church history, and second-confession stories.

Along the journey, we find that the history of the Bible is *messy*. This shouldn't surprise us because the birth of the incarnate God was also messy. Jesus, the Son of God who is also the Word of God, used very human means in both instances to reveal himself. But like Jesus' life on earth, the history of the Bible has God's unmistakable and sovereign hand on it from Genesis to Revelation.

If we ever get lost in this journey, we must turn back to Jesus, who is the cornerstone of our first and second confessions. The parallels between the incarnate and written Word are not just beautiful analogies—they are the keys to understanding truth.

As believers in the divinity of Christ, we collectively begin at this point of faith in agreeing that God entered humanity about two thousand years ago through the most unsuspecting means. Perhaps a teenager getting impregnated by the Holy Spirit and giving birth to God's Son in an obscure manger might seem as far-fetched as the Scriptures being birthed through the pens of men. And yet, knowing that that the former is true, there is much hope (and proof) that the latter is true as well.

1

The Scriptures and Salvation

HAVE YOU EVER ASKED GOD POINT-BLANK, "Is the Bible truly your Word?" This is one of the most important questions we can ask our Lord, and he will answer those who sincerely ask because that's just who he is. He is a God of clarity and a God of revelation. His answer might not come in a euphoric epiphany or an emotional experience, but his answer will come to those who sincerely ask.

I asked God that question after that fateful revelation in 2007 about my hidden unbelief. God initially led me in the form of inquisitiveness. A million other questions suddenly surfaced, questions I had never voiced before. Who wrote these individual books? When were they written? How do we know they are still in their original form? Who decided that these books would be compiled into one big book called the Bible? Are there other writings that didn't make the cut? Who translated them into other languages? The questions went on and on.

I realized that I had suppressed these questions mainly out of fear. I was afraid to ask these questions because I didn't want other Christians to think I was questioning the inerrancy of God's Word.[1] I was afraid to voice my unbelief. I was a Bible study leader and a respected member of the church by this point. I felt like I had a lot to lose by sharing my confusion and doubts. I was also afraid to ask these questions because they could prove my doubts about the truth of God's Word. It's one thing to disbelieve the veracity of Scripture based on cursory knowledge, but what if a thorough examination led to hard and undeniable *proof* that God's Word was a total fabrication? Then my faith would come tumbling down like a house of cards.

But it dawned on me that God *wanted* me to ask these questions. These questions did not offend or unsettle him. He invited and aroused these questions so I would know his Word better. So I would know *him* better.

EVEN SPIRITUAL GIANTS HAVE DOUBTS

Let's say that a person professed faith in Christ and then learned that a book in the Bible (for example, Esther) never mentions God directly throughout the whole book. And let's say this person doubts if Esther has a rightful place in the Bible, and then this person dies without resolving this query. Does this person get to spend eternity with Jesus? Absolutely. This person's salvation has been secured, even if they had doubts about the rightful place of Esther (or any other book) in the Bible. Now, did this person miss out on understanding more fully God's sovereignty and love for his people through the lives of Esther, Mordecai, Haman, and Xerxes? Absolutely, as well. But edification is separate from salvation.

This scenario was true of Martin Luther, the great sixteenth-century Reformer, with the book of James. Luther wanted to remove James from the Bible because he felt that it was "really an epistle of straw . . . for it has nothing of the nature of the

Gospel about it" and believed that the "epistle of James gives us much trouble." Luther was so frustrated with James that he called the author "Jimmy"! In Luther's own words, he stated, "I almost feel like throwing Jimmy into the stove."[2] I am generally hesitant to disagree with Luther, but I must part ways with him on this one.[3] I believe that the epistle of James highlights the gospel of Jesus with a nuance like none other. My main point is that few would doubt that Martin Luther is in God's presence at this very moment.

I want to reiterate this point because this book should never cause anyone to doubt one's salvation. If you have accepted Jesus as Lord and Savior, there is nothing, not even a limited knowledge of the Scriptures, that negates your salvation. Even if someone only believes the basic parts of the gospel, and then disregards many other parts of Scripture, this person's salvation is no less secure.[4]

Yet you might doubt the veracity of certain parts of Scripture; and perhaps doubt and confusion have set in in other areas of your life as well. It could be a fractured relationship, mounting bills, health concerns, or a relational rift that might make you wonder how your salvation intersects with the daily grind. You thought accepting Christ would solve your problems, but Jesus seems rather far off. You hear that he loves you, and you desperately want to believe this is true. But if you're honest, your soul feels cold. If your life seems confusing, imbalanced, or lacking in hope, God wants you to turn to his Word.

But why would you turn to his Word unless you know that it's truly from him? It can be a vicious cycle of grasping and hoping, doubting and wondering, and pondering how our relationship with Jesus can seem stunted in daily living. If so, the best place to run is to the Scriptures—even if you're unsure of its veracity. Read it, meditate on it, examine it, and pray it. Also *engage* with it, asking God to grant you the knowledge and faith to understand his Word. He will meet you on those pages and orchestrate divine appointments and thoughts to bring you to the truth of his Word. The Word of God promises what no other book can promise, because the Bible is God offering his own heart to us.

THE CANON

If we're honest, though, the Bible can be a daunting read. There are names that are very hard to pronounce, some stories leave us scratching our heads, and the historical divide between now and then can seem sizable. Names such as Shelumiel and Zurishaddai, tales such as Lot's wife turning into a pillar of salt, and historical actors such as pharaohs and prophets are a few examples. But this is when the craft of history can skillfully bridge the distance between times and cultures.

History can seem like entering time travel and landing in a foreign and unrelatable land. But knowing the history of the Bible is a powerful avenue to accepting God's Word as truth. One way to offset the divide is to start from the present and work backward when possible. Reverse chronological order allows us to begin together here in the twenty-first century, and then travel backward collectively. Reverse chronological order can also make the distant past not seem so distant. For example, two thousand years seems like a considerable divide, but the same period might seem more accessible when measured in life spans. If the average life span is seventy years, then thirty life spans (or even fewer, since lifespans generally overlap) covers two thousand years, bringing us back to the days of Jesus.[5]

History is also a helpful lens to analyze the claim that the books of the Bible are inspired by God. For Christians, the word *canon* is used to denote this claim. This means that the Bible we hold in our hands today is composed of the actual books that God inspired. Christians today can be certain that the Bible received from the Israelites in the Old Testament and Christians in the early church is truly God's Word. We believe with confidence that the books identified as authoritative and inspired were correctly received and accepted in these communities.[6]

So what does the term *canon* mean today? It's not a widely used term in common (meaning non-church, non-academic, or non-theological) language. You might know of a person with that name, or the company so named that makes printers, cameras, and such. Or the word might make you think of weaponry used for warfare way back when (that *cannon* has two n's). But when we use the word *canon* associated with the Protestant Bible, it refers to the sixty-six books of the Old and New Testaments, and *only those books*, as God's Word.[7] A mid-twentieth-century biblical scholar defined *canon* as writings "acknowledged by the Church as documents of the divine revelation."[8] In essence, these are the words God "breathed" into existence.[9]

The first time *canon* was used to denote divine revelation was in AD 367 by Athanasius, who held the important position as bishop of Alexandria.[10] In his annual letter circulated to his churches, Athanasius stated that "it seemed good to me . . . to set before you the books included in the Canon, and handed down, and accredited as Divine." Referencing the Old and New Testaments, Athanasius wanted to make sure that these books alone were counted as "divinely inspired Scripture" and not to "mix them up" with "the books termed apocryphal."[11] The books in the canon, then, are not words fabricated from human minds, but they are revelations from the eternal God. God selected human agents to convey his thoughts in writing, but they were conduits of these thoughts rather than the originators.

Further, the Latin and Greek etymologies of the word *canon* refer to a straight rod that could be a measuring stick. The extrapolation from this term can add a dual meaning, where canon also implies the absolute standard (or rule) from which all other standards should be measured. This means that in our post-(post-) modern world, the Bible claims that there is absolute truth and all other truths must bow and submit to the truth proclaimed in the Scriptures. There is no picking and choosing—the *entire* Bible and its teachings on money, forgiveness, homosexuality, divorce, and all other topics are accepted as the ultimate truth and authority.[12] All this to say, a twenty-first-century Protestant Christian is referring to the thirty-nine books in the Old Testament and twenty-seven in the New Testament when using the term *canon*.

When such a sizable claim is made in the realm of spiritual matters, people rightfully look to spiritual proof to authenticate the pronouncement. Golden tablets sent from celestial beings sure would be nice right about now to substantiate the divine nature of the Word. For Christians, however, there is no such tale. Instead, we must look at the messy nature of canonicity, while marveling at God's sovereign, divine, and expert hand in creating the Word. How can we bridge the messy with the marveling? One powerful method is by fusing history and theology—and praying that both types of information transform into faith.

Even if history proves that Jesus lived and died, historian Scot McKnight notes that "the historical method cannot prove . . . that Jesus died for our sins and was raised for our justification."[13] That is, even if historical evidence proves that Jesus died on a Roman cross, history alone cannot prove *why* Jesus hung on that cross. That's where theology comes in. Borrowing words from theologian Kevin Vanhoozer, "History alone cannot answer the question of what the canon finally is; theology alone can do that."[14] Discerning which books are actually considered divine in origin requires that historical information is distilled through a theological framework. A correct understanding of God's nature, attributes, and personality are a part of this quest of discernment. History and theology working in tandem help build our faith in Jesus who was sent to redeem us.

EXPERIENCING AND INVESTIGATING THE SCRIPTURES

Salvation is a mysterious thing, and the moment of salvation can be anything but a definable moment. There are the dramatic stories of conversion, but there are also those who grew up in Christian homes and somewhere along the way their parents' faith became their own. Although our Savior is always the same, our salvation stories are personal and nuanced. The same can be said of our relationship with the Scriptures.

My brother's story drives home this point. Henry, who is now a criminal prosecutor, previously found himself on the wrong side of the law. He made some poor choices as a teenager and ended up in jail. At a very low moment in his life, sitting in solitary confinement, he looked around his cell and saw a lone piece of literature: the Gospel of John. He wasn't a follower of Jesus, but desperation made him pick up this book. As he read, he felt a divine presence enter the room and into his soul. His reading of the Word made him believe in the possibility of God's existence—in the possibility that the divine and carnal intersect, that hope can be found in the most unexpected places.

This type of experiential interaction with the Word is certainly a gateway into knowing Jesus more, whether as Savior or the Word. Start there, whichever verse the Lord speaks to you. Hang on to that verse or passage for dear life, and then ask him to speak more through his Word. Along the way, continue to attend church, listen to sermons, join a Bible study, and read books that point to the formation and elucidation of Scripture.

My own journey, combining these elements, took many years. A pivotal moment came when I experienced the power of the Scriptures in a life-altering way. This was the year that Josephine, my daughter, was born, which turned out to be the hardest year of my life. A few months after giving birth I was diagnosed with a condition called a "petrous apex mucocele" that had gotten out of hand, and I lost hearing in my right ear and feeling on the right side of my face. My surgeon told me that I would eventually lose all hearing and all feeling if left untreated. After the diagnosis, I started having panic attacks, where even in broad daylight and open spaces I felt like I was drowning. Then I started feeling dizzy and blurry in my vision, and I went through more scans and tests than I can remember.

I was extremely fortunate to have a compassionate and skilled doctor who spent hours talking with me about all the options available. Doug and Julie, my pastor and his wife at our church in Woodland, California, walked alongside us every step, offering an incredible amount of prayer and counseling. Brian, my husband, was nothing short of heroic. But it was God's Word that broke through the madness.

One evening, I came across Scripture reminding me of God's love and sovereignty. Those words felt like lightning entering my soul, and I wept and laughed in unison. In that moment, I felt a divine joy, sustaining peace, and deep cleansing of my soul that can't be fully explained in human vernacular. It felt like a light had dawned in pitch darkness.

I savored the words and meditated on them, praying them over my soul. Those verses ushered me to meditate on God's character and how much he loves me and is so worthy of being trusted. And eventually my fears about my surgery and all the what-ifs slowly receded.

Each fear based on a what-if was replaced with God's holy presence and promise. What if I can't take care of my newborn? *God loves Josephine more than I do and will care for her regardless.* What if the surgery is a failure and I lose all hearing and feeling on that side? *God formed me in my mother's womb, continues to sustain my every breath, and is mindful of my frame.* What if I don't survive the surgery because of some accident? *God knows the exact moment of my last breath on this planet, and nothing can thwart his best and loving plans for my life. He is sovereign, he is good, and he is so very much in love with me.*

Soon after that experience, I asked God, "How did all this come together? And how did your Word become what it is?" I heard nothing right away, but soon after, a friend recommended that I read New Testament scholar F. F. Bruce's *The Canon of Scripture*.[15] I had started digging around for answers for over a year at this point, but Bruce's book was like none other. From defining the term *canon*, to covering the compilation of both the Old and New Testaments, Bruce's book served as a textbook of sorts. From there, God stoked a love for his Word, both in content and canonicity.

God's Word entered my soul like lightning. But this moment was not singular. It sparked a lifetime of delving into the Scriptures, where newfound discoveries awakened greater love for the Bible. But it has also brought me to deeper wrestling with Scripture, where certain verses have left me confused or certain parables remain enigmatic. I explore the hard questions, not in order to believe that the Bible is truly God's Word, but because I already believe by faith and reason that it is.

CIRCULAR REASONING

In college I had a lab partner in biology class who was an atheist, but we often talked about God. I was a new Christian, and I just couldn't help bringing up Jesus from time to time. He was so actively working in my life that it was difficult not to talk about him. One day my lab partner, James, said, "Where are you getting all this stuff about Jesus?" and I replied, "The Bible." He then said, "How do you know it's true?" And I told him that the Bible declares that it is the Word of God. I pulled out my pocket Bible and pointed to John 1:1. He then asked me, "Can you prove that it's the Bible without referencing the Bible?" And I told him, "Hmm, well, uh . . . let me get back to you on that."

I wish I could contact James now and share with him what I've learned since. Yes, there is much evidence that the Bible is God's Word. Yes, you can make this claim without referencing the Bible. It takes faith to believe the reality of this claim, but it also takes faith to disbelieve it. Rejecting a claim needs a framework and rational basis, too, and it takes faith to discount the truth of the Scriptures. I hope that professing Christians, as well as atheists like James, will discover the evidence outside of Scripture that the Bible is indeed what it claims to be: God's Word to humanity.

Christians have been taught that faith comes by hearing, and hearing by the word of God, as stated in Romans 10:17. Many powerful verses throughout the Bible attest to its own veracity, and I believe every one of them (for example, Deuteronomy 8:3; Psalm 18:30; Psalm 19:7; Matthew 4:4; John 1:1; Ephesians 6:17; 2 Timothy 3:16; Hebrews 4:12; 2 Peter 3:16). But citing its own claim can seem, at best, circular reasoning, and, at worst, fraudulent. There are many well-respected theologians who would disagree with me on this point. For example, theologian and authors Norman L. Geisler and William E. Nix believe that using the Bible to validate its own assertion for holy status is not circular reasoning and any such charges are "unfounded."[16] Many good books already exist using Scripture to validate Scripture, and there is a place and need for such dialogue. This book, however, aims to use mainly nonbiblical sources to prove why Scripture should be accepted as God's Word.

Using Scripture to validate Scripture can seem like a version of, "We can prove that Zeus exists because Hermes believed in Zeus's existence." This does not mean, however, that Scripture will be excluded in our discussion in what it *self-proclaims*. The Bible claims to be God's Word, and it is vital that we examine these assertions. We'll also assess the Scriptures alongside historical evidence and theological and rational dialogue.

I respect James's question and these challenges because they are rational and important assertions. The Christian faith is making a gigantic ask of its followers to base their entire lives on words written centuries past. There are easy parts to believe—such as loving our neighbor and serving the poor—but what about the passages about not judging others and forgiving those who have hurt us? The Bible is not a buffet where we can pick and choose various parts to conform to our taste. It must *all* be true; otherwise the claim of canonicity in sum total cannot be made.

Faith comes by hearing God's Word, and there is no doubt about that. As you read about canonicity, my prayer is that you would continue to study and consume the Scriptures voraciously. May our investigation into the compilation of God's Word be coupled with his actual Word. May the Lord open our hearts and minds to the truth of the Word as we delve further. We cannot trust and live out the Scriptures apart from the Holy Spirit, so to the living God we ask,

Holy Spirit,

We need you. And we invite you to take charge of this journey. May the words in this book point to the Scriptures. And may the Scriptures illuminate our hearts and minds to your eternal love. In Jesus' name we pray, Amen.

QUESTIONS TO PONDER

1. Where are you currently on the journey from the first to the second confession?

2. What has your relationship with the Bible been like?

2

Old Testament Tradition

OUR FAMILY HAS A TRADITION where we pray every time we get in the car to leave for an event. Josephine and JD anticipate praying soon after we've buckled up; they will ask, "Aren't we going to pray?" if we haven't prayed yet after covering a half mile from our house. We often ask the Lord for safety, blessings for the people we will meet, and for our hearts to be attuned to his leading. And this is probably a good tradition for me since I drive a teensy bit faster sometimes than I should.

Your family might have a tradition, too, whether it's daily or seasonal. Traditions can be symbolic, important, comforting, or just plain fun. Traditions have a way of pointing us back to something important. Some traditions, however, are not always worth keeping and should rightfully be jettisoned. The weightier the tradition, the more we should examine the rite, especially since the inheritors of tradition might not always understand its relevance or value.

For Protestants, we have inherited a rich tradition from the Jewish religion mainly in the form of the Hebrew Bible. (For our purposes, when we use the term *Hebrew Bible*, we're referring to the Masoretic Text, which is the official version of the Hebrew Bible [Old Testament] for Judaism and Christianity.[1]) Our Old

Testament is arranged in a different order from the Hebrew version, but its contents are identical. The key difference is that Protestants interpret the text differently than the Jewish tradition. Both attest to a Savior who will deliver humankind from the cesspool of sin, but Protestants believe that Jesus is this very Savior, while Jews do not. Messianic Jews are in a separate category, as they hail from Jewish roots and also believe that Jesus is Lord and Savior.

The Hebrew Bible comprises twenty-four books, categorized into three divisions. There is great likelihood that the earliest version of the Hebrew Bible had two divisions (the Law and the Prophets), but the threefold division has been the standard since ancient times.[2]

* Division 1: The Law (some other names are Torah, Pentateuch, Books of Moses) includes five books: Genesis, Exodus, Leviticus, Numbers, and Deuteronomy.

* Division 2: The Prophets, subdivided into the Former Prophets and Latter Prophets, includes eight books.

  + Former Prophets include Joshua, Judges, Samuel and Kings.

  + Latter Prophets include Isaiah, Jeremiah, Ezekiel, and the Book of the Twelve Prophets (also called the Minor Prophets).

* Division 3: The Writings includes eleven books. The first three are the poetical books—Psalms, Job, and Proverbs; the next five are called the Scrolls (also known as Megilloth) and include Ruth, Song of Songs, Ecclesiastes, Lamentations, and Esther; and last are Daniel, Ezra-Nehemiah (in one book), and Chronicles, which comprise the historical books.

If we extrapolate these three divisions into lists, they are arranged like this:

1. Genesis

2. Exodus

3. Leviticus

4. Numbers

5. Deuteronomy

6. Joshua

7. Judges

8. Samuel

9. Kings

10. Isaiah

11. Jeremiah

12. Ezekiel

13. The Book of the Twelve Prophets (Hosea, Joel, Amos, Obadiah, Jonah, Micah, Nahum, Habakkuk, Zephaniah, Haggai, Zechariah, Malachi)

14. Psalms

15. Proverbs

16. Job

17. Song of Songs

18. Ruth

19. Lamentations

20. Ecclesiastes

21. Esther

22. Daniel

23. Ezra-Nehemiah

24. Chronicles

THE LAW

The first division of the Old Testament is often labeled as the Pentateuch, for the five books (*penta* meaning "five"): Genesis, Exodus, Leviticus, Numbers, and Deuteronomy. The word *Pentateuch* comes from the Greek word *pentateuchos*, which refers to the "five scrolls," and was first popularized by the Hellenized Jews living in first-century Alexandria.[3] To be "Hellenized" meant adopting Greek practices, such as speaking the Greek language and adopting Greek culture. It would be like when my family immigrated from South Korea to the United States many years ago and became "Americanized." We spoke "Kon-glish" (a combination of Korean and English) and celebrated Thanksgiving with traditional fare such as turkey and stuffing but added buchimgae (Korean pancakes), mandoo (dumplings), and kimchee (spicy fermented vegetables).

The fusion of two cultures allows the best, and often the most convenient and expedient, forms of society to blend. One salient example of such fusion within Jewish Hellenization is the Septuagint, which is the Hebrew Bible translated into Greek, starting from the third century BC.[4]

The Pentateuch is also called the *Torah* in the Hebrew language, which means "instruction" in holiness. Such instructions are found within the laws and covenant often attributed to Moses. Hence *The Books of Moses* and *The Law* are other designations for this set of books. These names point to the prominent position given to the Pentateuch as the first group of books considered as divinely inspired by God.

While Christians proclaim that *all* Scripture is equally divine, the Pentateuch holds special prominence as the *first* of the three divisions in both order and authority. The Pentateuch, or the Law, is considered the most foundational part of the Hebrew canon and always comes first in the Old Testament canon, preceding the Prophets and the Writings. Order is significant here.

Although the Pentateuch consists of five distinct books, they tell one unified story about creation, sin, and covenant. Some scholars believe that the Pentateuch should be divided into two sections: Genesis 1–11 and Genesis 12–Deuteronomy 34. The first part covers the creation of the world, people being made in God's image (*imago Dei*), and the fall of humankind when sin entered into the world. The second part explains God's covenant promise of redemption to Abraham and his descendants (the Israelites).

The primacy of the Pentateuch naturally raises the question about authorship. Who wrote the Pentateuch? Moses has largely been attributed as the author of the Pentateuch, although there is ongoing discussion about this assertion. Jerome, the early church father, proposed that perhaps Ezra the Priest authored the Pentateuch. There has been much debate and dialogue, especially in the last four hundred years, about authorship. One interesting contention with the Moses authorship is language. Some argue that Moses could not have written the Pentateuch, much less in Hebrew, stating that the Hebrew language did not exist during Moses' time, which is largely considered to be around the thirteenth century BC.[5] The Hebrew language derived from the Phoenician alphabet, and the first evidence of the Hebrew language purportedly dates to the tenth century BC, after the Israelites entered Canaan.[6] Moses unfortunately never made it into the land of Canaan, as the Bible itself attests (Numbers 20:12).

Many esteemed Christians still believe in Moses' authorship, however. John Calvin stated that Moses has "established the credibility" of writing the Pentateuch, which is "the design of Moses, or rather of the Holy Spirit, who has spoken by his mouth."[7] Many scholars believe that Moses authored portions of the Pentateuch while others believe that he served more as an editor-at-large rather than the primary human agent for inscribing the contents.[8] Even though writing flourished and became more commonplace after the eighth century BC, this doesn't mean that writing did not exist prior to this period.[9] Clay seals and short inscriptions reveal that writing existed in Canaan before the nation of Israel was born, which is dated possibly during the Middle Bronze period (c. 2000–1750 BC).[10] Also, the Israelites' ancestors could have used an earlier Canaanite script that later developed into the Hebrew language.[11]

The New Testament, and specifically the recorded words of Jesus, further shed light on this subject. In John 5, Jesus said to the Jews who "persecuted him" for "doing these things [such as healing] on the Sabbath" (v. 16): "But do not think I will accuse you before the Father. Your accuser is Moses, on whom your hopes are set. If you believed Moses, you would believe me, for he wrote about me." (vv. 45-46). Jesus mentions a sizable number of other passages from the Pentateuch as well. Along with the Psalms and Isaiah, Jesus referenced the Pentateuch often. His teachings often mentioned the law of Moses, in an effort to show the Pharisees how they had wrongfully understood the Mosaic laws. And when Jesus was tempted in the wilderness, he quoted from Deuteronomy 8:3, stating that "man does not live on bread alone but on every word that comes from the mouth of the LORD."[12]

This is a lot of information to digest about authorship! And this is just the tip of the historical and scholarly iceberg. Much has been written about whether Moses could have written about his own death (Deuteronomy 34) or if the world's "humblest man" would have self-declared such a thing (Numbers 12:3).[13] Others believe that most of the Pentateuch survived in oral tradition until Joshua, Moses' successor, or Eleazar the priest inscribed these words in the Hebrew language.

There truly is no end to the theories about proper authorship regarding the Torah.[14] But the point is that the ambiguities of authorship did not seem to perplex the Jews of the first century. For them, the laws of Moses, or the Pentateuch, were sacred and divinely inspired words from God sent through Moses. This is the tradition that Protestants have inherited from the Jews regarding the laws.

THE PROPHETS AND THE WRITINGS

The order of the books in the Former Prophets (Joshua, Judges, Samuel, and Kings) was established, just like the ones in the Pentateuch.[15] Starting from the Latter Prophets, however, the order of these books, and those in the Writings, have not been so firmly fixed. The sequential fluidity seemingly stems from two reasons: first, the narrative in these books follows no distinct chronological progression; and second, the writings were on separate scrolls, not bound in book format, and with no directions for ordering. The use of codices (scrolls stitched together to form a book) began in the first century AD, during the era of the early Christian church.[16]

Before then, these scrolls were held together in a container, with no specification for order or sequencing.[17]

Joshua picked up Moses' mantle, and the natural transition to this book and then to Judges, Samuel, and Kings (of which the latter two are not subdivided as in the Protestant Old Testament) unfold the Israelites' story of entering, possessing, and then backsliding in the Promised Land. These books in the Former Prophets are followed by the four books in the Latter Prophets, so named to denote the sequence of prophets who provided clarion voices to Israel during their rise and fall. The last book in the Latter Prophets, the Book of the Twelve Prophets, is also known as the "Minor Prophets." Minor doesn't mean less important here—it just denotes the shorter length of these books compared to the major ones.

The last division, The Writings, contains the most controversial books of the Old Testament canon.[18] Though the book of Psalms has been an unquestioned part of the Hebrew canon, other books on this list have been the subject of scrutiny and contention. For example, there is no definitive evidence that Jesus and his contemporaries accepted Esther, Ecclesiastes, and the Song of Songs as Scripture; but also there is no proof to show that these books were excluded from what first-century Jews would have considered divine revelation.[19] Church father Athanasius omitted Esther from his canonical list in the fourth century AD, and some of the earliest Syriac Old Testament copies do not include Esther, Ezra-Nehemiah, and Chronicles.[20] These fluctuations in scope, order, and organization were ongoing from the time of the early church, as shown, for example, when Josephus appended Ruth to the end of Judges and Lamentations to Jeremiah. Each book in question is addressed in the coming chapters.

Still, this overall three-part Hebrew canon was considered a tradition by Jesus' time. Writings that date to the second century BC suggest that the threefold Hebrew canon existed in this form at least a century before Jesus' birth. Jeshua Ben Sira wrote a "book of wisdom" that was translated by his grandson in 132 BC. In this translation, the grandson mentions often that his venerated grandfather studied "the law and the prophets and the other books of our fathers."[21] Terminology, however, can be a little tricky as "the law and the prophets" can denote the whole Hebrew Old Testament, and Sira's grandson could have been mentioning that his grandfather studied the whole Jewish Scriptures as well as other Jewish writings. Or, as the wording suggests, he was stating that his grandfather studied the Hebrew Bible in these three parts.

There is other evidence that Jesus and his contemporaries accepted this three-part Hebrew canon as Scripture. The inclusion of Chronicles as the last book of the Hebrew canon leads to one plausible theory.[22] When Jesus mentions "the blood of Abel to the blood of Zechariah" in Luke 11:51, he might have been mentioning the first and last martyrs mentioned in the Jewish Scriptures. Abel was murdered by his brother Cain (Genesis 4:8), and Zechariah, who was probably the son of Jehoiada, was stoned to death for speaking against the king (2 Chronicles 24:20-22). In this first-to-last setup, Jesus could have been referring to those whose innocent lives were taken from the first pages of Scripture to the last, according to the Jewish canon. Hence, Genesis and Chronicles would have bookended the Hebrew Bible.

THE BIBLE THAT JESUS READ

Did Jesus and his contemporaries read *this* version of the Hebrew Bible, from Genesis to Chronicles? We don't know the definitive answer to this question, and there is no hard proof as to some of the books (e.g., Esther, Ecclesiastes, and the Song of Songs) and their order (outside of the Pentateuch and the Former Prophets) that comprised what Jesus meant by the Scriptures as a whole. But the uncertainty of these points does not compromise the integrity of the Old Testament message. The main message of the Hebrew Bible—from creation to the forming of God's people, the Israelites, and the issuing of God's covenant promises (Noah, Moses, Abraham, and David)—is clear throughout the Hebrew Bible. And Jesus and his contemporaries inherited these scrolls as sacred tradition and sacred writings.

The greatest proof to this claim would be to look at Jesus' enemies, the very people who crucified him. They looked for any and every reason to indict him of heresy. They paid people to wrongly accuse Jesus on false charges. Yet not once did they question Jesus' appeal to the Scriptures. On Jesus' frequent references to the Scriptures, even his opponents seemed to agree on the sacredness of the texts under discussion. They didn't say "Which Scripture?" or "You're citing from heretical texts!" or anything along those lines.

When Jesus and his apostles engaged in religious debates with their opponents, they all appealed to and agreed on what was meant by "the Scriptures" and the authoritative position it held in Jewish life. There were outliers who deviated from the larger Jewish tradition—for example, the Samaritans included only the Pentateuch in their Bible, and the Sadducees might have omitted Daniel due to references of a resurrection—but a vast majority of first-century Jews believed in the Hebrew Bible as the Word of God. The authority of these texts and the "near unanimity" is astounding among such "diverse groups" of people.[23]

JEWISH TRADITION

If we believe in Jesus, then we must believe what he believed. And he believed in the Scriptures. Chapter three gets into *what* the Scriptures constitute, but *that* the Scriptures were front and center in Jesus' identity cannot be discounted. Jesus the Jewish man inherited the Scriptures, and Jesus the Son of God came to fulfill these Scriptures.

Jewish tradition is critical in our examination of the Christian faith since Jesus was a Jew, hailing from the lineage of Judah. The church was initially composed of Jews who came to believe that Jesus is indeed the Messiah, and Jesus came to fulfill the Jewish laws, not to abolish them (Matthew 5:17). God birthed Christianity out of the Jewish tradition, and the Old Testament comprises the writings of this rich inheritance.

The Hebrew Bible and the Protestant Old Testament are one and the same. There are differences in the ways they *interpret* these words, but whether fixed in twenty-four books (the Hebrew Bible) or thirty-nine (the Protestant Old Testament), and despite different sequencing, the contents of these writings are unvarying.[24] The *TaNaKh*, which is an acronym for *Torah* (the Law), *Nevi'im* (the prophets), and *Ketuvim* (the Writings), served as the foundation of Jesus' ministry and the birth of Christianity.

Jesus' references to the Old Testament abounded throughout his ministry. Protestants today are not "People of the Book," as the Puritans were called, because of humanistic tradition; the Christian faith imitates the one that Jesus founded, which was built on the Scriptures. Jesus' ministry was predicated on citing, explaining, and illuminating the Old Testament writings. His ministry was one of the Word, one that claimed that he was the long-awaited Messiah and the fulfillment of all Scripture. He is the light of the world (John 8:12), just as he is the light of the Word. If we are true followers of Christ, we must also be people of the Scriptures and torchbearers of this light. There is no other way.

QUESTIONS TO PONDER

1. What is an important tradition you have inherited?

2. How did Jesus both honor and challenge Jewish traditions?

3

A Timeline of
the Old Testament

WHO TOLD YOU that the Bible is God's Word? Do you trust this
person with your life? The person who asserted this claim probably
has some credibility with you, if not some influence and perhaps
even authority. This person is asking you to base your entire life
on this assertion. But relationships shift, and people disappoint.
Unless we know for sure *personally* that the Bible is God's Word, our
trust in the Scriptures will ebb and flow based on human relationships and cultural trends. Our worldview, morals, and conduct—
the way we spend money, have or abstain from sex, and engage in
relationships—must conform to the Bible if it is God's actual
message to humankind.

Whether you received your first Bible as a gift or purchased it
yourself, you may have had a sense of holding something holy.
The term *holy* means dedicated to God or something set apart for
religious purposes. I remember feeling a weightiness of the Bible—
its holiness—when I received it as a gift the night I accepted Jesus
as my Lord and Savior. I knew I was holding something sacred,
something connected to that incredible feeling I had when Jesus
entered into my heart.

Then I opened the Bible. Genealogies, lots of blood, murder, sordid tales, redeeming love and faithfulness—and that was just in the first several chapters of Genesis! I was overwhelmed. To be honest, some of the stories in there confused me. Did God really tell Abraham to kill his own son? Even if God didn't let him go through with it, that was unsettling. Did Jonah *really* go into the belly of a great fish? Even if it was a super gigantic whale, I just couldn't imagine that. The many other supernatural stories of parting seas, walking through fire unscathed, and miraculous healings made me start to categorize the Bible into sections. There were the "for sure it's true" portions, then the "perhaps it's allegorical" or "I'll never understand this" sections, and then the "maybe it slipped in by mistake" parts. I never voiced these categories, but the Bible started to fissure in my mind.

Despite these thoughts, I still felt its holiness. But I also felt stuck. I knew that Jesus was my Lord and Savior, but how does the Bible *really* relate to him? And how does it relate to *my life*?

When I started reading the Bible, I was in my first serious relationship, and it was a really bad one. I was a high school senior, and he was a junior at a nearby university. At this point in my life, so many of my boundaries had been violated that I didn't even know what they were. And I unfortunately didn't know how to say no when it counted. After reading the Bible, I was even more confused about this relationship. Did the Bible require that I marry him or break up with him? I wasn't so sure. All I knew was that I felt so much shame and that the holiness of the Bible reconfirmed the fact that I was living a life not consistent with its commands. The relationship ended when he disappeared into a world of gambling, but my confusion and fears remained.

As a new Christian, some parts of the Bible seemed rigid and somewhat discordant with the feelings of love and acceptance I felt in Jesus' presence. I veered toward passages on love and forgiveness, and I steered clear of much of the Old Testament because it seemed harsh. Thankfully I started attending a church that taught the Bible systematically. Week after week, I acquired more Bible knowledge; the progress seemed like droplets in the ocean, but at least my faith didn't seem bone dry.

Then my faith was bolstered in the most unexpected place—an undergraduate history class. I began my freshman year at UC Berkeley the fall after my first confession, and something that a well-respected history professor said stunned me. He discussed the *Epic of Gilgamesh*, a tale from ancient Mesopotamia. I was fascinated to learn that this epic poem, written in the Akkadian language, included a flood account that resembles the one mentioned in Genesis. I could not believe that a biblical account as significant as Noah's ark and the flood was found in *extra*biblical sources, outside the Bible.[1]

Were there other ancient sources that corroborated stories in the Bible? It seemed like it, and I wanted to find out. I was thinking of majoring in history, but to be honest I was very intimidated. Everything in the past seemed so distant and foreign, and I wasn't sure if I could track. Eventually I did major in history because the stories were so compelling, but I felt like I had plunged into the ocean with no life vest or swimming skills. I was deluged with questions about how my newfound faith intersected with my fascination with the past.

ROOTED IN HISTORY

One of my first questions concerned time. How far back does the Bible go? Genesis 1 starts "in the beginning," and I was curious as to when this beginning began. I soon discovered that the creation account has many viewpoints. There is no consensus regarding the age of the earth or how to interpret the "days" of creation.[2] Even the church fathers differed in their viewpoints, as do scholars today.[3] Mostly, I was surprised to find out that leading Christian scholars differ on their interpretation of the creation account but still remain orthodox in their theology. This reminds me of the adage, "In essentials, unity; in non-essentials, liberty; in all things, charity."[4] What impressed me the most was that thoughtful Christianity doesn't dictate blind conformity. Each theory has reasons behind its assertions. While some seem more reasonable than others, I was intrigued by the dialogue that went behind these theories.

The events in the Garden of Eden are hard to pinpoint in terms of time frame, but some archaeological evidence comports with the biblical account. The rivers Tigris and Euphrates mentioned in Genesis 2:10-14 are inferred as the current-day rivers so named in Assyria. The rivers Pishon and Gihon are harder to deduce, but satellite imagery shows that the "land of Cush" (known as current-day Ethiopia and the Horn of Africa) had "two major rivers" that "once flowed from west-central and southwestern Arabia into the Persian Gulf region." Though these riverbeds are now dry, their tracks can be seen running through "Dilmun," which interestingly is known as a paradise akin to Eden in ancient Near East literature.[5]

All good stories include a memorable location, such as Narnia and Middle-earth. The Bible is no exception. Unlike these fantasy lands, however, the Bible references real places that still bear witness to the narratives revealed from Genesis to Malachi. Syro-Palestine (modern-day Israel, Jordan, Lebanon, and Syria) constitutes about 80 percent of the history that unfolds in the Old Testament. The other 20 percent include ancient Mesopotamia (modern-day Iraq and Iran), Asia Minor (modern-day Turkey), Egypt, and the Arabian Peninsula (currently controlled mostly by Saudi Arabia). Collectively these territories are known as the ancient Near East, or today as the Middle East.[6] And like Narnia and Middle-earth, the notoriety of the Middle East cannot be discounted. The reverberations of this region are felt throughout the world; the tensions that exist today find their start in biblical times.

While the Old Testament was written in the course of about one thousand years, the story it tells covers a longer time span. The preexilic period (events before the Babylonian exile in 586–538 BC) focuses on the land of Canaan, starting with the patriarchal narratives. Starting in Genesis 12 with the call of Abram (whose name is changed to Abraham in Genesis 17), this time is generally dated to the Middle Bronze I (c. 2000–1900 BC) and Middle Bronze IIA (c. 1850–1750 BC) periods.[7] Most historical sources date the Israelites' exodus from Egypt to about the thirteenth century BC,[8] and big transformations occurred during the patriarchal period. For example, Mesopotamia transitioned largely from a semi-sedentary society to more of a settled one. This meant that more fortified cities and permanent structures were built toward the end of the Middle Bronze IIA period. The sparsely populated lands that Abraham encountered and the general lifestyles recorded in the Bible comport with the archaeological findings during this era.[9]

A QUICK HISTORY LESSON

For many years, whenever I saw *BC* in literature, I often glossed over the dates and labeled the event as merely "super old."

Whether it was 4 BC or 400 BC, it all seemed the same. Rationally I understood that many things change over a course of four hundred years, but from a twenty-first-century vantage point, it all seemed about the same. It reminds me of when I was a kid and anyone between twenty-five and fifty years old pretty much looked the same. Unless you were a senior citizen, you were just in the "old" category (senior citizens were in the "super old" category). Now that I'm in the throes of middle age, the age distinctions look a lot more nuanced!

Distinctions between generations, even old ones, are noteworthy. Imagine where twenty-first-century moderns would be about four hundred years ago (versus four years ago). For Americans, they would land on the shores of Plymouth along with the Pilgrims in 1620 (versus the latest technological or political shift in the last four years). These comparisons remind us that much can change in varying timespans, even the old ones. Though a day is like a thousand years and a thousand years as a day to the Lord, he also knows about the significant changes that occur during these timespans.

Let's get some history terminology under our belts. When *BC* is used, it denotes "before Christ," and *AD* refers to *anno Domini*, which means "in the year of the Lord" in Latin. Human history has kept time by the birth of Christ, even if people believed in his divinity or not. Some academics have replaced BC with BCE (Before the Common Era) and AD with CE (Common Era) in the last few centuries. For this book, I'll keep to the terminologies used for thousands of years and adhere to BC and AD.

Although the whole premise of the BC/AD delineation is to mark Jesus' birth, there is some discrepancy. In fact, 4 BC is most likely the year that Christ was born.[10] While a few years is a minor timespan in the grand scope of human history, Christians should note that Jesus most likely was not born on December 25 in the year AD 1 according to the Gregorian calendar! Also, events that date this far back usually have a *c.* to denote *circa*, which means "approximate dates."

Understanding historical timelines can be tricky, especially the BC part. We all know that 1914 (WWI) occurred before 1944 (D-day), meaning that 1944 (the bigger number) is more recent. But the opposite holds true for BC dates. The year 332 BC (when Alexander the Great invaded Egypt) occurred *before* 44 BC (the assassination of Julius Caesar), meaning that 44 BC is more recent than 332 BC.

Finally, when someone says "the twentieth century," they are referring to the 1900s. This is true because the years AD 1 to 99 span the first century AD, and then the years AD 100 to 199 comprise the second century AD, and so on. Therefore, the years AD 1900 to 1999 comprise the twentieth century AD. For BC, the same principle holds true. For example, 150 BC falls in the second century BC, and 250 BC falls in the third century BC. This might seem elementary, but it's helpful to remember when dates start filling our timeline.

LOCATION AND TIMESPAN

The Genesis narratives continue through the time of Joseph, when he brought Jacob and his relatives to live in Egypt. Some sources date this event to c. 1875 BC, which begins the time known as the "Egyptian Period." Several hundred years elapsed between Genesis and Exodus, and a time came when the new Pharaoh was not familiar with Joseph and his ancestors.[11] This was the time of great hardship for the Israelites noted in Exodus 1–2. From here, the story progresses to the exodus, when Moses led the Israelites out of Egypt and into their Promised Land.

There are two dates, the early and late, for the exodus journey out of Egypt. Working backward, Moses' interactions with the pharaohs of Egypt could have been either between c. 1500–1425 BC (early) or c. 1318–1237 BC (late).[12] If we track with the early date, this means that Moses' Egyptian mother could have been Hatshepsut (Jochebed was his actual mother); Thutmose III (c. 1504–1450 BC) was the Pharaoh who sought to kill Moses; and Amenophis II (c. 1450–1425) was the Pharaoh during the exodus.[13] These dates, both in their estimation and conjecture, show that reasonable historical theories can be formed for biblical events.

From the exodus, the Israelites marched into the desert during the fifteenth century BC and remained there for forty years (c. 1447–1407 BC). They entered the land of Canaan near the turn of the fourteenth century BC, and then entered into the Period of the Judges (c. 1360–1084 BC). The dizzying downward cycle of disobedience, oppression, repentance, and deliverance lasted for about 280 years.[14] The last judge, Samuel, anointed Israel's first king, Saul, whose kingdom began c. 1051 BC, and lasted until David became king. The twelve tribes of Israel continued on under one king until 931 BC, when the ten tribes in the north became "Israel" and the two southern tribes of Judah and Benjamin remained loyal to the house of David and became known as "Judah." This divided monarchy lasted from c. 931–586 BC.

During this time the Assyrians conquered the northern tribes with the fall of Samaria in 722 BC. The Assyrians also tried to conquer the southern tribes in 701 and 688 BC but were unable to. Judah existed as a vassal state of Assyria until the Babylonians ascended. Under Nebuchadnezzar's reign, the Jews encountered the Babylonian exile. And in 586 BC the beautiful temple that Solomon had built was destroyed by the Babylonians.

The Babylonian rule ended when the Medo-Persian Empire ascended in 539 BC. After Babylon's fall, Cyrus the Great, the Persian king, let the Jews return to Judah c. 537 BC. During this time the Second Temple was built in Jerusalem under the leadership of Ezra, Nehemiah, and Zerubbabel, and the Jews had a modicum of independence. The Old Testament era came to a close around 400 BC with the prophet Malachi, for whom the last book of the Protestant Old Testament book is named.[15]

These dates are important. But as stand-alones they do little to convince someone to love the Scriptures. They relay a historical framework important to truth-telling. And without them, it's easy to view the Bible alongside the Narnia or Middle-earth stories, rather than as true narratives rooted in history. These dates, however, become meaningful when Christians read the Bible accounts of all the stories mentioned. When these dates come alongside the reading of Scripture, there is a synergistic effect that takes place. The stories in the Bible take center stage, and these historical dates are like the surrounding props that bring additional fullness to the narratives—and we see that history has often corroborated Scripture. Whether the early or late dates of the exodus are correct is less important than that a plausible timeframe exists. Real historical actors lived and breathed, and the biblical stories narrate God's plan unfolding amid a time-space continuum in which we are included.

ALWAYS BACK TO JESUS

Along our journey, if things seem confusing or complicated, the best place to return to is Jesus. And the question to ask is, What does this text say about Jesus and the message he proclaimed? For example, the story about Jonah and the whale could seem far-fetched, except that Jesus mentions it specifically in Matthew 12. He says in verse 40, "For as Jonah was three days and three nights in the belly of a huge fish, so the Son of Man will be three days and three nights in the heart of the earth." For those of us who are followers of Jesus, we believe that there is a Creator God who spoke the world into existence by his very words; and we believe that Jesus *resurrected* from the dead. Then it should not be so hard to believe that our timeless God allowed a prophet to detour a few days in the belly of a whale before going to Nineveh—both to share the message of God's love with the Ninevites and to foretell the kind of resurrection that the incarnate God would demonstrate to the world.

Like Jonah, Abraham was selected by God to make a point—a big point. This time, God chose this key patriarch to highlight faith. In Genesis 22, God tests Abraham by asking him to sacrifice his only son, Isaac. Thankfully Abraham never had to go through with the sacrifice since God sent an "angel of the LORD" to stop him, and this riveting story ends happily with an unhurt Isaac. This story would be incomplete and perhaps confusing without a window into Abraham's mind revealed in Hebrews 11:19: "Abraham reasoned that God could even raise the dead, and so in a manner of speaking he did receive Isaac back from death." This passage means that Abraham, even as he pulled the knife out to kill Isaac, had faith that God is a God of the *resurrection* and would fulfill his promise to populate the world through Abraham's descendants.

Has God put another person in the belly of a whale for three days or asked another parent to sacrifice his son? The answer is an emphatic no. These special circumstances in the Bible masterfully weave the Old and New Testaments to tell one story about none other than Jesus. He alone is the focal point of all Scripture and the lens through which all claims of canonicity must be filtered.

As Christians, we believe that one day all people will stand before Jesus and face whether we believe him to be Lord, liar, or lunatic (what is known as the trilemma).[16] For those who are on the journey trying to answer this question, there is much credibility that the writings that attest to Christ's divinity have been faithfully preserved as canonical. If an all-powerful and all-knowing God can orchestrate whales to swallow up prophets and send angels to stay the hand of murderers, then surely he can faithfully preserve the *logos*, the Word, that he spoke to humanity.

QUESTIONS TO PONDER

1. What is your favorite Old Testament book, and why?

2. How does knowing the historical timeline of the Old Testament affect the way you read Old Testament narratives?

4

A Close-Up of
the Old Testament

EVANGELIST BILLY GRAHAM was in his early thirties and found
himself at Forest Home, a retreat center in Southern California,
where he was a speaker at the College Briefing Conference. At this
point, Graham was weary and confused when he reluctantly accepted Henrietta Mears's invitation to speak at this conference.
Mears was the head of the conference and fondly referred to
simply as "Teacher." Graham noted her contagious enthusiasm
for the Lord and was drawn to her "faith in the integrity of the
Scriptures" as well as her understanding of "Bible truth" and
modern scholarship.[1]

Graham could not help but notice the disparity between
Ms. Mears and his good friend and preaching partner Chuck
Templeton, who had recently resigned as a pastor and enrolled in
Princeton Theological Seminary. Templeton's studies made him
doubt the foundations of Christian faith, "particularly concerning
the authority of the Scriptures." And Graham's deep respect and
affection for Templeton made it so that "whatever troubled him
troubled [Graham] also."[2]

Billy Graham felt caught between the worlds of Mears and
Templeton. He stated simply, "My very faith was under siege."

At this point, Graham, like Templeton, wrestled with the inspiration of Scripture. And Graham felt "a little hypocritical" about his uncertainties concerning the inspiration of the Scriptures and began an intensive study. He consumed the writings of theologians and scholars, and engaged in careful study of the Bible.[3]

In the midst of all this searching, he accepted the invitation to speak at Forest Home in the summer of 1949. After the daily events concluded, alone in his room one night, Graham opened the Bible and wondered "was the Bible completely true?" He stated, "I had no doubts concerning the deity of Jesus Christ or the validity of the Gospel" but as to the rest of the Scriptures, "I was certainly disturbed" if "not exactly doubtful."[4]

One night during the conference, Graham left his room to go for a walk. And under a moonlit sky on the Forest Home retreat grounds he dropped to his knees and opened the Bible "at random on a tree stump." Billy Graham describes this pivotal moment like this:

> The exact wording of my prayer is beyond recall, but it must have echoed my thoughts: "O God! There are many things in this book I do not understand. There are many problems with it for which I have no solution. There are many seeming contradictions. There are some areas in it that do not seem to correlate with modern science . . ." At last the Holy Spirit freed me to say it. "Father, I am going to accept this as Thy Word—by *faith*! I'm going to allow faith to go beyond my intellectual questions and doubts, and I will believe this to be Your inspired Word." When I got up from my knees at Forest Home that August night, my eyes stung with tears. I

sensed the presence and power of God as I had not sensed it in months.[5]

You might be where Billy Graham stood before he made his tree stump confession. Somewhere in your heart, you believe that the Scriptures are God's Word, but doubts remain. Perhaps it's been months, or even years since you've sensed the presence and power of God that Graham described. I hope that you'll be encouraged to know that a new world opened up for Billy Graham after he made his tree stump confession—what I would call his second confession.

The next day, Graham preached at Forest Home and four hundred people committed to following Jesus. Mears noted that Graham "preached with authority" undetected before.[6] Later that same year, newspaper tycoon William Randolph Hearst allowed the Los Angeles campaign to headline both in the *Los Angeles Examiner* and *Los Angeles Herald Express*. This favor bestowed on Graham allowed publicity on an unknown scale, which translated into mass conversions during this campaign, including Louis Zamperini's confession of faith in Christ.[7]

Some might say that Graham's newfound authority and influence in preaching after the tree stump prayer was sheer coincidence. Graham would disagree, and so does Will Graham, grandson of Billy Graham. The younger Graham notes: "Because of that moment kneeling by a stump at Forest Home, I get to hear stories of lives changed through my grandfather's ministry. Because of that moment, my father and I are invited around the world to share the same hope of Christ that my grandfather preached in Los Angeles. . . . That moment not only changed Billy Graham's ministry. It impacted eternity."[8]

WHAT'S IN FOR SURE

Billy Graham's story encourages me. Doubt can grip anyone, even the best of us. But Graham models for us what can be done when we're confused about the Scriptures. His intentionality in studying various theological claims and wrestling with the Bible itself during this time of confusion are noteworthy. Like Billy Graham, my prayer is that we would, by faith and reason, vigorously evaluate the Scriptures and its claims until a decision is firmly rendered.

The best way to assess the veracity of the Scriptures is to look at each book and also include books that failed to get canonized. There is no shortcut in studying the Scriptures, and some parts are labor intensive! But knowledge is power, and God encourages us to seek this kind of empowering. We read in 2 Peter 1:5, "Applying all diligence, in your faith supply moral excellence, and in your moral excellence, knowledge" (NASB 1995). In this passage, knowledge is listed in succession as an important Christian virtue, and without knowledge a vital element is missing in our faith journey. I pray that all of our diligence in seeking this knowledge will result in nothing short of "brotherly kindness" and "love," the two elements that conclude this list.

Acquiring new terminology is helpful in our quest to increase biblical knowledge, and these three words categorize the books of Scripture in question: *Homologoumena* (ho-mo-low-goo-men-uh), *Antilegomena* (an-ti-luh-gaw-min-uh), and *Pseudepigrapha* (soo-duh-pig-ruh-fuh). Yes, they're mouthfuls! But it'll be worth knowing what these terms describe.[9] Both the Old and New Testaments have their respective lists of books that fall under Homologoumena, Antilegomena, and Pseudepigrapha.

* Homologoumena are books unquestionably included in the canon and never disputed subsequently.

* Antilegomena are books initially classified as canonical but later disputed.

* Pseudepigrapha are books religious in nature but never included in the canon.

* Additionally, the Old Testament Apocrypha are books added to the Greek Septuagint but never included in the Hebrew Old Testament (discussed in chapter seven).

Books categorized as Old Testament Homologoumena are covered in this chapter, and those grouped as Old Testament Antilegomena, Pseudepigraph, and Apocrypha are discussed in subsequent chapters.

Let's start with good news. Out of the thirty-nine books in the Protestant Old Testament, thirty-four are considered Homologoumena. That means that only five books are considered Antilegomena (Esther, Proverbs, Ecclesiastes, Song of Solomon, and Ezekiel). And that means that nearly 90 percent of the Old Testament canon has never been disputed since the beginning of biblical writing. Since these books have never been challenged, there is no need to delve into each regarding canonicity. Still, it's helpful to know what they are, who were the purported authors, and the dates of coverage of events or inscription. They, along with the books labeled Old Testament Antilegomena, are listed here:

THE LAW (TORAH OR PENTATEUCH)

❋ Genesis

   ✦ Author: Moses, traditionally, since Genesis is considered one unit, along with the Torah or Pentateuch, but the book itself does not self-identify an author

   ✦ Chronology: events from creation to c. 1600 BC with the death of Joseph[10]

❋ Exodus

   ✦ Author: Moses, according to Jewish and Christian tradition

   ✦ Chronology: events from Joseph's death c. 1600 BC to Israel's encampment at Sinai in either 1440 BC or 1260 BC[11]

❋ Leviticus

   ✦ Author: Moses, according to Jewish and Christian tradition; natural assumption that Moses authored Leviticus as the phrase "the LORD said to Moses" is found over twenty-five times in this book[12]

   ✦ Chronology: some believe in an early date of inscription (1400 BC, during the first half of the Late Bronze Age); others place this at a later date (c. 1200 BC, during the early Iron Age)[13]

❋ Numbers

   ✦ Author: Moses, according to Christian and Jewish tradition; only one mention of Moses as author in this book (Numbers 33:2), but the phrase "and the LORD said to Moses" recorded in nearly every chapter; textual implications that priests were also recording and preserving instructions (e.g., Numbers 5:23)[14]

✦ Chronology: most likely written in the fifteenth or thirteen century BC, during the forty-year period in the desert[15]

✳ Deuteronomy

  ✦ Author: Moses[16]

  ✦ Chronology: written in mid-second millennium during the final weeks while the Israelites were encamped east of the Jordan[17]

THE PROPHETS

Former Prophets

✳ Joshua

  ✦ Author: perhaps authored by Joshua or passed down in oral tradition until written during the time of Samuel[18]

  ✦ Chronology: events took place either at the end of the fifteenth century or in the thirteenth century BC, from the beginning of the Israelites entering into Canaan through the death of Joshua[19]

✳ Judges

  ✦ Author: unknown, although Jewish tradition states that Samuel is the author

  ✦ Chronology: events covering several centuries, c. fourteenth through the eleventh centuries BC[20]

✳ 1 and 2 Samuel

  ✦ Author: unknown, but Hebrew tradition refers to these as the books of Samuel because of his important role in establishing Israel's monarchy

- ✦ Chronology: events from the end of the judges through the reigns of Saul and David, around the last half of the eleventh century and early part of the tenth century BC[21]

✳ 1 and 2 Kings

- ✦ Author: unknown, but Jewish tradition attributes the books to Jeremiah the prophet[22]
- ✦ Chronology: events spanning several hundred years, starting with the death of David c. 970 BC to the exile of Judah in 586 BC[23]

Latter Prophets

✳ Isaiah

- ✦ Author: Isaiah[24]
- ✦ Chronology: c. 740–687 BC (dates of prophetic activity)[25]

✳ Jeremiah[26]

- ✦ Author: Jeremiah, although Baruch was the scribe (36:4)[27]
- ✦ Chronology: c. 627–585 BC (dates of prophetic activity)[28]

✳ Ezekiel—Antilegomena (see chapter six)

- ✦ Author: Ezekiel
- ✦ Chronology: c. 571–562 BC (dates of prophetic ministry)[29]

The Book of the Twelve Prophets ("Minor Prophets"). Dates listed refer to dates of events or prophetic activity:

✳ Hosea

- ✦ Author: Hosea, son of Beeri[30]
- ✦ Chronology: c. 758–722 BC (dates of prophetic activity)[31]

✳ Joel

✦ Author: Joel[32]

✦ Chronology: unknown, with a wide variety of dates from the ninth to the second centuries BC[33]

✳ Amos

✦ Author: Amos

✦ Chronology: traditionally dated to the middle-to-latter years of Jeroboam II's reign (c. 760 BC)[34]

✳ Obadiah

✦ Author: Obadiah

✦ Chronology: traditionally dated to c. 586 BC, just after the fall of Jerusalem; but Obadiah's oracles have been dated from anywhere between 850 to 400 BC[35]

✳ Jonah

✦ Author: unknown, although the information from the book is taken from Jonah's account[36]

✦ Chronology: Jonah lived in the eighth century BC, although the dating of the book is uncertain[37]

✳ Micah

✦ Author: Micah

✦ Chronology: Micah prophesied during the reigns of Jotham, Ahaz, and Hezekiah (last half of the eighth century BC)[38]

✳ Nahum

✦ Author: Nahum

+ Chronology: sometime before the fall of Nineveh in 612 BC[39]

* Habakkuk

+ Author: Habakkuk

+ Chronology: c. 612–599 BC, before Babylon attacked Jerusalem[40]

* Zephaniah

+ Author: Zephaniah

+ Chronology: c. 640–609 BC, during the reign of Josiah[41]

* Haggai

+ Author: Haggai

+ Chronology: c. 521–486 BC, during the reign of Darius I, King of Persia[42]

* Zechariah

+ Author: Zechariah

+ Chronology: c. 520–early 400s, contemporary of Haggai and King Darius's reign (c. 521–486 BC) of Persia[43]

* Malachi

+ Author: Malachi

+ Chronology: unknown, but c. 460 BC (just prior to the reforms of Ezra and Nehemiah)[44]

THE WRITINGS

Poetical Books

* Psalms

  + Author: many authors, such as David (who wrote seventy-three of the psalms), Asaph, Moses, Solomon, Heman, Ethan, and the Sons of Korah[45]

  + Chronology: inscribed from the early monarchy (c. 1000 BC) to after the exile (c. 400 BC)[46]

* Job

  + Author: unknown

  + Chronology: events traditionally dated to the patriarchal period, as Job's lifestyle and mention of the roving Sabaeans and Chaldeans (Job 1:15, 17) reflects this era[47]

* Proverbs—Antilegomena (see chapter six)

  + Author: various authors, including Solomon, Agur, Lemuel of Massa, anonymous writers

  + Chronology: inscribed during the time of Solomon (c. 970–930 BC) and on; most likely anywhere between the tenth century BC to the sixth century BC[48]

Five Rolls (Megilloth)

* Ruth

  + Author: unknown[49]

  + Chronology: events during the decades surrounding c. 1100 BC[50]

* Song of Songs—Antilegomena (see chapter six)

  + Author: anonymous

  + Chronology: early preexilic period[51]

* Ecclesiastes—Antilegomena (see chapter six)

  + Author: unknown[52]

  + Chronology: composition date widely varies from the third or fourth century BC to the seventh or eighth century BC[53]

* Lamentations

  + Author: unknown, Jewish tradition and the Septuagint identify Jeremiah as the author[54]

  + Chronology: unknown date of composition, but the text suggests that the book was written soon after the fall of Jerusalem c. 586 BC[55]

* Esther—Antilegomena (see chapter five)

  + Author: anonymous

  + Chronology: most likely composed in the fourth or late fifth century BC[56]

Historical Books

* Daniel

  + Author: Daniel[57]

  + Chronology: presumed to be written in the sixth century BC (c. 520 BC)[58]

* Ezra-Nehemiah

  + Author: anonymous, but Jewish tradition (Babylonian Talmud: *Baba Bathra* 15a) identifies Ezra as the author[59]

+ Chronology: historical coverage spans the first return from Babylonian exile (c. 539 BC) to the end of the fifth century BC, with special focus on the reign of Artaxerxes of Persia (458–430 BC)[60]; actual composition of these books probably completed c. 400 BC[61]

* 1 and 2 Chronicles

+ Author: unknown, although some older scholarship and Jewish tradition (based on the Babylonian Talmud: *Baba Bathra* 15a) have identified Ezra as the chronicler[62]

+ Chronology: genealogy dates to Adam in the Garden of Eden, but narrative starts with David's reign over Judah (c. 1000 BC) to Cyrus's decree (c. 539 BC)[63]

These Homologoumena books were recognized as canonical early on and no later than the intertestamental period and certainly during New Testament times; and descriptions of "holy" and "the Holy Scriptures" were likely attached to these writings.[64] Location further authenticated their sacred status. Inspired writings were initially kept in the Ark of the Covenant (the Ten Commandments, Deuteronomy 10:2[65]) or near it (the Law, Deuteronomy 31:24-26). And later the Book of the Law was kept in the temple that Solomon had built (2 Kings 22:8).

Only sacred writings considered canonical were given such a privileged holding place. It would be like the *Mona Lisa*, *The Wedding at Cana*, and other valuable art today that are placed under tight security. Although I consider my children's art invaluable, the Louvre would not spend the money and energy in safeguarding their art. In the same way, writings that weren't deemed sacred would not be placed in the temple. These thirty-four books of the Old Testament Homologoumena were all safeguarded in the temple, which was considered a "sacred library" for these holy texts.[66]

TWO MINUTES AT A TIME

Would you consider going back to this list of OT books and picking one to delve into for the next week or two? It can be a two-minute read per day—an idea that comes from a story I heard from a dear friend, Chris. He recently told us how he fell in love with the Scriptures two minutes at a time, and his story is a powerful reminder that God can do much with the best that we can bring to him.

Chris worked construction many years ago, so he was an early riser. He befriended a Christian who challenged him to keep his morning routine the same with one exception: put his Bible next to the coffeemaker. So Chris woke up at 4:30 a.m. as usual, showered, got dressed, and then headed to the coffee machine. And he read God's Word for two minutes as he drank his morning brew. Those two minutes generally turned out to include about ten to fifteen verses. His friend then challenged him to change one additional thing: don't turn on the radio on the drive to work, but think about and talk to God about what he read. Within months Chris fell in love with the Scriptures, and his love for Jesus and his Word continue to inspire many.

I hope that ten or fifteen verses daily, or however many needed to feed our souls, will provide light for our journeys. I also hope the historical backdrop to these books, in their authorship and timeframe, might give you a sense of firmer footing.

For those who are in church ministry, I hope Billy Graham's story will alleviate some guilt and bolster your faith. You might resonate with Graham's journey, where he found himself deep in ministry before fully embracing the entirety of the Bible as God's Word.

Before his tree stump prayer, he had already gained recognition as America's then-youngest college president and as an evangelist with Youth for Christ. He had also held "Billy Graham Crusades" in various cities such as Charlotte, Grand Rapids, and Altoona and preached in various places in post-WWII Europe. Despite all this, Billy Graham had not yet fully made his second confession.[67]

Just as Graham asked, "Could I trust in the Bible?"[68]—perhaps that's the question on your heart. This very question is a gift from God. That any of us could even articulate such a question means that a watershed moment is at hand. No more relativism, no more back and forth, and no more lukewarm living. Either hot or cold, one must choose whether the Bible is what it claims to be. In 2 Timothy 3:16 we read that "All Scripture is God-breathed." The Bible claims that God literally breathed these words into existence for the teaching and illumination of his people. Graham intensely wrestled with his faith and doubts that fateful evening, honestly praying and wondering if he could take God at his Word—the entirety of it. Though Graham didn't have everything figured out, he knew enough to make his second confession that fateful night in 1949.

We don't have to know the Bible inside and out to believe that it's all true. I'm so thankful for that because I have a long way to go in my theological journey. But like Billy Graham, I want to continue to come to God honestly, knowing that his loving arms are opened wide and he invites us to come just as we are.

QUESTIONS TO PONDER

1. Are there any similarities between Billy Graham's journey to making the second confession and your journey?

2. What is your biggest intellectual hurdle in making the second confession?

5

Reading Esther:
A Case Study

SHE IS BEAUTIFUL—DROP-DEAD GORGEOUS. And she knows how to use her beauty and body to gain the attention of important men. She's kept her identity as a government subversive a secret, and her duplicity has worked. She soon finds herself as a sexual partner of the most powerful man in the land. Is this moral? Does it matter when the stakes are so high? She uses this insider-privilege because mayhem is about to be unleashed on her people. This woman is Esther from the Old Testament.

If you've been attending church for a while, perhaps you've heard a sermon or two on Esther. And most preachers note that God is never mentioned in the book of Esther—at least not explicitly. For this reason, Esther was labeled as one of the five writings in the Old Testament Antilegomena (Ecclesiastes, Esther, Ezekiel, Proverbs, and Song of Solomon)—books that were originally included in the Hebrew Bible, but subsequently up for debate regarding canonicity. The book of Esther was eventually deemed canonical and serves as a perfect example of how each book of the Bible has undergone a thorough and rigorous examination. Esther is singled out in this chapter to show that context—which is vitally important when reading the Scriptures— and careful examination of the Scriptures go hand-in-hand.

As a refresher: all of the books of the Law are in the Homologoumena, and all of the books in the Prophets, minus one (Ezekiel) are also in the Homologoumena. This means that four out of the five books categorized as Old Testament Antilegomena come from the Writings.

Further, three out of these Antilegomena books come from the Five Rolls known as the Megilloth.[1] It's worth examining, then, what the Megilloth represents and why the books in this subdivision have been the subject of so many debates. Chapter six examines four of these five books, and one (Esther) is covered in this chapter. For now, let's pause and gain another helpful study tool in understanding distinctions in the Bible: hermeneutics.

WHAT IS HERMENEUTICS?

Hermeneutics (pronounced "her-me-noo-tics") is the art and science of interpreting Scripture. Hermeneutics means that we read the Bible as it was intended to be understood in the proper context. The Greek word *hermēneuein* means "to explain, interpret or to translate," and those who engage in hermeneutics do exactly that. This means that hermeneutics lets the reader discern what the author intended to communicate, understanding that interpretation can never exist in a vacuum; there are presuppositions and cultural contexts for all that we read.[2]

Context means everything. We contextualize our world all the time, although we might not be aware of it. For example, we read different sections of the newspaper with different expectations. My children and I often read the comic section after having breakfast on Sundays, and we know that the message in *Baby Blues* (our favorite comic) is different from the sports section (Go Dodgers!). In the same way, prophecy in the Bible, for example, *should* have different expectations from the Five Rolls (Megilloth).

Let's discuss context in another way. Have you ever said, "I'm so hungry, I could eat anything!"? Obviously, you didn't mean *anything*. You didn't mean, "I'm so hungry, I could eat a phone, stapler, tires on the car, etc." That would be preposterous. You meant, "I'm so hungry, I could eat *any type of food*." You could mean sushi, pasta, nachos, or In-N-Out Burger. At least that's what I would mean. In the same way, context is incredibly important when we look at the Bible.

One example could be when Jesus commands his followers to hate their own father, mother, children, and so on (Luke 14:26). Jesus did not mean to straight-out hate these people whom he repeatedly commanded to love, forgive, serve, and honor. Proper hermeneutics contextualizes this statement in *relation* to how much we're supposed to love God. When our hearts are fully given to him and we love God with everything we've got, all other loves pale in comparison.

One major aspect of hermeneutics concerns intended meanings as they relate to genres of writing, or writing style. The human authors for each book of the Bible employed specific literary styles. Just because a book is in the Bible doesn't mean that every book is in the same genre of writing. The Bible stands alone and is undoubtedly in a class all by itself, but like all literary works it must be categorized in its proper genre. Because the Bible is compiled of sixty-six books, it makes sense to divide these books into proper genres (and the Hebrew divisions of these books are incredibly helpful in denoting how these books should be read on a macro level and when engaging in Bible studies verse-by-verse).

The Old Testament made a lot more sense when it was ordered in its original divisions found in the Hebrew Bible. When the Hebrew Bible was compiled, the books were placed in a threefold division, an important distinction.[3] A big reason for doing so was hermeneutics, although the creation of the Hebrew Bible obviously predates this term.

Protestant Bibles rarely have categorized divisions, except the large division between the Old and New Testaments. I humbly suggest that categories (the Law, Prophets, and Writings) be inserted, or at the least be recognized and understood. These subdivisions are like a flashlight providing illumination in the dark. If you ever felt lost in understanding the Old Testament, reading it in these subdivisions will be a critical and helpful first step in understanding the Bible in its proper context.[4]

MEGILLOTH

We can practice hermeneutics on Esther, so let's start with the genre of writing. What was the author's intent in writing Esther? Was it actually intended to be a historical account of the Jews? Or was it written as historical fiction to inspire moral and spiritual lessons? Some academics believe Esther falls somewhere between these two possibilities, with fact and fiction commingled. I disagree with this assertion and believe that Esther is an accurate historical account during the Persian Empire, especially given that no historical evidence has ever been found to contradict its claims.[5] But this does not mean that Esther was intended primarily to be a work of history. The writing style suggests that Esther was meant to be more narrative than history.[6]

How should we categorize Esther? If you walk into your local bookstore, you won't look for a cookbook in the fiction section. In the same way, Esther is not categorized with the historical books according to the Hebrew Bible. The setting of this story is just one generation before the events in Ezra-Nehemiah, yet Esther was not placed alongside these historical books, as it is in the Protestant Bible.

Also Esther *reads* altogether differently from these strictly historical narratives. Humor and irony are replete throughout Esther, and historical discourse is not the primary agenda. It's not a surprise, then, that the Jewish elders did not place Esther in the historical section of the Hebrew Bible, but, rather, this book was labeled as Megilloth.[7]

The *Megilloth* is also known as the "five festival scrolls" or simply as the "Festival Scrolls." And these books, or scrolls, were read aloud annually during the following Jewish festivals:

* Purim (Esther)[8]

* Fast of Ab (Lamentations)

* Passover (Song of Solomon)

* Pentecost (Ruth)

* Tabernacles (Ecclesiastes)[9]

What types of writings are read out loud? Hopefully interesting ones! We've all listened to speakers who have lost our interest, despite our valiant efforts to pay attention—and these types of speakers are probably not invited back. To be given the honor of holding an annual address means that the material is extremely interesting and meaningful. Each of the books above certainly fill that description.

The way something is conveyed makes a world of difference. Let's use the Bible to fill in this point. A part of the Bible reads like this:

Then Moses stretched out his hand over the sea, and all that night the Lord drove the sea back with a strong east wind and turned it into dry land. The waters were divided, and the Israelites went through the sea on dry ground, with a wall of water on their right and on their left. (Exodus 14:21-22)

Now let's compare this description with another one:

By the blast of your nostrils
  the waters piled up.
The surging waters stood up like a wall;
  the deep waters congealed in the heart of the sea.
. . . terror and dread will fall on them.
By the power of your arm
  they will be as still as a stone—
until your people pass by, Lord,
  until the people you bought pass by. (Exodus 15:8, 16)

Both are referencing the same event; and while both are undoubtedly interesting, the latter is more theatrical. Both are historically accurate, but the latter is what was read or sung aloud after the exodus from Egypt. In the same way, the book of Esther should be viewed in the same theatrical light and with the understanding that allegory does not preclude historical accuracy.

Three of the five books of the Megilloth are labeled as Antilegomena, and this is important. These festival scrolls were never intended to be primarily works of history, and to assume so is like putting a round peg in a square hole. Esther was purposefully written in short-story format, which greatly aided in keeping the listeners' attention. The theatrics, however, never lessened or compromised the historical accuracy of the tale.[10]

The next time you read the Old Testament, remember where these books were originally used in the Jewish culture. God's Word is God's Word no matter what. But God has a repertoire; he is incredibly consistent in speaking to his children, but sometimes he speaks through thunder and other times through a gentle wind. God is not monotone, but creative and nuanced in communicating his heart to his beloved children.

ESTHER

God's creativity and nuance are highlighted throughout the book of Esther. Esther is read aloud annually at the Jewish festival known as the Feast of Purim in late February/early March to celebrate victory over enemies.[11] *Purim*, which means "lots," fittingly bespeaks of chance. Like casting lots, there is an element of chance encounters and mere happenstance that could be construed throughout Esther's story. There are no angelic appearances or deliverances in God's name—God's name is not mentioned a single time throughout the entire story.

God's seeming absence has caused angst and debates for the church fathers and subsequent generations. The canonical status of the book of Esther has also been questioned for other reasons, foremost being the argument that historical sources seemingly do not mention key characters such as Vashti, Esther, Mordecai, and Haman.[12] But both of these concerns are actually opportunities to see that faith and reason, belief and research go hand-in-hand.

Esther's story unfolds in the Persian Empire during the middle of the fifth century BC. There have been unfounded theories that Mordecai authored this book, but the general consensus is that the author remains anonymous.[13] On the throne was Xerxes I (who was also known as Ahasuerus), the son of Darius I (who was also known as Darius the Great). Xerxes reigned from 486–465 BC, and the book of Esther was most likely written down in the fourth to perhaps late fifth century BC.[14]

With the obvious exception of Xerxes, there are no extant historical sources that seemingly include other characters mentioned in the book of Esther. The Greek historian, Herodotus, was a contemporary of Xerxes and his son, Artaxerxes; and Herodotus mentions the adventures and accomplishments of Queen Amestris, wife of Xerxes, but there is no such mention of Vashti or Esther. Some historians, however, believe that "Esther" could have been a shortened and abbreviated name for "Amestris," although that's a far stretch.[15] Also, Persian texts from the last years of Darius I or early years of Xerxes I include a government official named "Marduka," which could have been "Mordecai."[16] Even if these name extrapolations are inaccurate and Esther and Mordecai remained unnamed in historical sources, the absence of their mention does not mean they did not exist. New historical evidence can always be discovered, and "arguments from silence" can never convincingly prove nonexistence.[17]

The most seriously debated issue about Esther concerns God's seeming absence. He isn't mentioned a single time—not by name, not in prayer, and not by implication. God's people are undoubtedly delivered from evil, but who gets the credit? Mordecai and Esther played their cards right and seemingly a whole lot of luck—or chance, like purim—factored into the Israelites' victory. But did God orchestrate these events? Although God's name is absent from this narrative, his fingerprints and sovereignty are unmistakably seen throughout.

Also, it is interesting and exciting that the name of Jehovah (YHWH) is seen *four* times in acrostic form in this book. Scholars have noted that the fourfold inclusion of this acrostic in such a short book makes it "beyond the realm of mere probability" and too frequent for coincidence.[18] In addition to these four, there is one acrostic of "EHYH" ("I AM that I AM") inserted in this book as well. And in three ancient manuscripts, these five acrostics are written in majuscular form, which means they are written purposefully in larger script so that they stand out "boldly and prominently."[19]

Esther was a controversial book among the early church fathers, and the Septuagint version of Esther (which includes additional chapters not included in the Protestant canon) only added to the confusion. So much more can be said about Esther—especially how God often seems silent in our lives and yet is working mightily all around us.

Understanding Esther in its rightful context helps me relate more to this story. The book of Esther isn't a history lesson, it's an invitation to understand God's heart—and that's reassuring because personally this book has both encouraged and saddened me. I am encouraged because the villain is defeated, retribution is served, and the Jews are delivered from annihilation. But as a woman, I've struggled with Queen Vashti being disposed like yesterday's trash and with Esther spending an obscene amount of time beautifying herself to sexually satisfy Ahasuerus, even if he was a king. Recently, though, I've realized that it wasn't just the women who suffered sexually. The many eunuchs who are mentioned all suffered too.[20] Perhaps some of their names are recorded to give them a place of recognition: Mehuman, Biztha, Harbona, Bigtha, Abagtha, Zethar, and Karkas (Esther 1:10), and

Hegai, the king's eunuch in charge of the harem (Esther 2:3). These men, alongside Esther (also known as Hadassah), are known by name to us and certainly by their Creator. The eunuchs' suffering doesn't lessen the pain for the concubines or deposed queen, but this story reveals that God's redemption and favor can be found in the most unexpected places (Esther 2:9, 2:15, 2:17, 5:2, 5:8). God's care for the least of us, men and women alike, shows us that he is enough even in our fallen world.

As we end this chapter, may I invite you to read the book of Esther anew, while asking the Lord to speak into your life? I'll do the same. Let's ask the Lord to speak through this ancient text and bring light and redemption to a time such as this.

QUESTIONS TO PONDER

1. Has the Lord spoken to you through the book of Esther? If so, what did you learn or discern about yourself, the Lord, and/or your circumstances?

2. How does reading the Old Testament books in their original Hebrew division help set better expectations in learning from the Bible?

6

Disputed Books of the Old Testament

My HUSBAND, BRIAN, sings beautifully and can pick up most musical instruments in no time. I, on the other hand, am tone-deaf. One of my favorite quotes comes from Ulysses S. Grant, who was also tone-deaf, who once said, "I only know two tunes. One is Yankee Doodle, and the other *isn't*."[1] You might know someone who is also tone-deaf, whether musically or otherwise. They're out of pitch, out of tune. They seem off-key, whether in song or in life.

When we read the Bible, it's vitally important that we hear the right tune, that we read the words in the right context (and practice good hermeneutics). Otherwise, we won't be able to tune ourselves to the truth of the Scriptures. As we continue to study the books labeled as Old Testament Antilegomena, I pray that we would be in awe of God's tone, the interweaving of prose and poetry, drama and suspense, and his love that is the steady beat behind it all.

SONG OF SOLOMON

I remember carefully sidestepping the Song of Solomon during devotions with the kids when they were younger. I wasn't prepared to explain the verses about arousal, undressing, and breasts (especially those likened to fawns, verses 4:5; 5:3-4). The many other passages about the lover's intoxicating fragrance, lips dripping with honey, and awakening of love made me quietly hope that they wouldn't stumble upon these passages before they turned (at least) double digits. The Jewish tradition, however, does the exact opposite by purposefully choosing this book to be read—out loud! During the Jewish Passover feast, this book has been incorporated into the annual celebration to remind the Israelites of God's love for them.

This book undoubtedly has sensual elements, but this was not problematic nor was its canonicity questioned in the Jewish tradition in the years before Christ. The Song of Solomon (also known as the "Song of Songs" or simply "Songs") has been a long-standing part of the Hebrew Bible.[2] Just how old this book, or poem, is cannot be pinned down with accuracy. Persian influence can be traced in the depiction of the "great lover," but some of the language also suggests Aramaic and Greek features. That's why a generous timeframe of the early preexilic period is generally attributed to the date of composition.[3]

This book is traditionally attributed to Solomon, but the wording from the opening line, "The Song of Songs, which is Solomon's," can be interpreted as *by, to, for,* or *about* Solomon. Because of the ambiguity, most credible sources will state that the authorship should remain anonymous.[4] For the Israelites, this book was less about sensual love and more about God's passionate love for them. God's love—which is all-consuming, altogether satisfying, beautiful and mystical—is worthy of poetry and song.

In the first century AD some Jewish leaders pondered if the book was too erotic to be holy. But this questioning about canonicity surfaced long after the Jewish tradition had confirmed its place in the Hebrew Bible—and at least a millennia after its composition. The first to raise doubt was Shammai, who was an important first-century Jewish scholar. But Rabbi Akiba ben Joseph (c. AD 50–132) quickly put any confusion to rest. Rabbi Akiba, who was the first-century leading Jewish scholar and given the title of "sage" for his unusual wisdom, answered any doubt by stating, "All the ages are not worth the day on which the Song of Songs was given to Israel; for all the Writings are holy, but the Song of Songs is the Holy of Holies."[5] These strong words put to rest any doubt about these love poems' rightful place in the canon. And this simple debate, among others regarding the Old Testament Antilegomena, show that the Song of Solomon was unlike the hotly contested books, such as Esther, in the Antilegomena.[6]

ECCLESIASTES

If the Song of Solomon seemed too sensual, then Ecclesiastes raised concerns because it seemed too skeptical. The rabbinic school of Shammai first raised this point starting in the middle of the second century AD, but none of their interpretations were substantive enough to warrant real doubt.[7] Ecclesiastes holds a long tradition of being included in the Hebrew Bible, and fragments from this book were discovered among the Qumran scrolls.[8] Also, although there are no direct quotes from this Old Testament book, it appears the New Testament (for example, Romans 8:20 and James 4:14) refers to Ecclesiastes in thought and language.[9]

The author of this book remains anonymous. He self-identifies as "Qoheleth," and this Hebrew word can be extrapolated as "teacher" or "preacher." The author also self-references as a "son of David," but there is no definitive proof that Solomon wrote this.[10] David had many sons, and any descendant of David could have easily and rightfully called himself son. The composition date widely varies from the seventh or eighth century BC to the third or fourth century BC, depending on how the Greek and Persian influences are interpreted. Martin Luther influenced a generation of scholars who have subscribed a postexilic date (c. 300–200 BC) to Ecclesiastes, while the more traditional viewpoint cites a preexilic date of composition.[11]

Ecclesiastes was read at the Feast of Tabernacles, which is considered Israel's most joyous feast. It might seem odd to use a "skeptical" poem for such a happy celebration, but the Jews never considered this book to be one of cynicism or doubt. The many passages about enjoying life and God's blessings would resonate well with this annual celebration. And the exhortation to eat and drink and find satisfaction in life—not merely for fun but realizing it's a "gift of God" (3:13)—makes this the perfect book for such an occasion.

The word *vanity* or *meaningless* (found thirty-eight times) is translated from the Hebrew word *hebel*, which literally means "breath." Like the fleeting vapor of one's breath, the author mused about the empty pursuits of life.[12] While these raw and unfiltered musings can suggest cynicism, these points of honesty never undercut the final answer: fear God and keep his commandments. By doing so, true fulfillment in life may be found.

PROVERBS

Billy Graham stated, "By reading five Psalms and one chapter of Proverbs daily, you will be able to read them through each month. The Psalms will tell you how to get along with God, and the Proverbs will tell you how to get along with your fellow man."[13] In the last few years, I've imitated Graham by reading five psalms and one proverb daily. I mostly started this practice because I desperately needed encouragement (Psalms) and wisdom (Proverbs). I deeply desire to do both better and find myself in these books almost daily.

Psalms and Proverbs are both in the Poetical Books within The Writings in the Hebrew Bible. But unlike the book of Psalms (which Jesus quoted from often and categorized as Homologoumena), Proverbs was labeled as Antilegomena. The reason for this categorization, though, is brief and straightforward. The only real issue with Proverbs stemmed from verses that seemed to contradict one another. For example, Proverbs 26 includes two such verses in succession:

* "Do not answer a fool according to his folly, or you yourself will be just like him." (v. 4)

* "Answer a fool according to his folly, or he will be wise in his own eyes." (v. 5)

A few Jewish leaders thought these verses contradicted one another, making the book illogical.[14] The leading Jewish rabbis responded with this answer: sometimes you have to put a fool in his or her place with a word or two, and other times it's better to ignore the fool.[15] This concern was not a serious or long-standing one, and the deep-rooted tradition of Proverbs being accepted in the Hebrew Bible was not much disturbed by this consideration. In fact, Proverbs was considered canonical before the second century BC, and many additional sources, including the Dead Sea Scrolls, categorized this book as Scripture.[16]

Many commentaries on Proverbs focus on authorship (Solomon being the most prominent among the sages of Israel), the date of compilation (anywhere between the tenth to sixth century BC), and the universal nature of wisdom.[17] Proverbs includes almost no Hebrew history, which makes the book even more applicable across time and culture.

EZEKIEL

All of the books in the Old Testament Antilegomena are categorized among "the Writings" in the Hebrew Bible, but Ezekiel is the exception. Written by the prophet Ezekiel, this book is categorized among the Latter Prophets. Ezekiel was one of the 10,000 Israelites taken into Babylonian captivity in the late sixth century BC, and his position as a God-sent prophet was never in question.[18]

The book of Ezekiel was always included in the Hebrew Bible, but later Jewish scholars raised questions about canonicity. At the heart of the issue was Ezekiel's understanding of temple rituals and supposed anti-Mosaic teachings. For example, these Jewish scholars were concerned that Ezekiel 46:6 prescribed a young bull, six lambs, and a ram for the New Moon festival, but Numbers 28:11 required two young bulls, one ram, and seven male lambs a year old.

Once again, context is vital. Chapters 40 through 48 of Ezekiel focus on the millennial age and the temple to be built after the Tribulation. Ezekiel was writing to God's people while in exile, using symbolic and figurative language to paint a future day of redemption. As those in exile, the Israelites sorely needed a reminder that a better future awaited them—one where they would worship God in spirit and in truth. Ezekiel used symbols (such as animal sacrifice, temple rites, and measurements for temple courts) to prophesy of that better day coming and to encourage God's people to not lose heart while held captive in a foreign land.

Ezekiel used prophetic language to encourage the homesick Israelites, rather than to provide architectural plans for temple construction or specific directions for animal sacrifice. And he never intended for the specifications in these chapters to be taken literally.[19] This temple would be unlike any other, one where "The LORD Is There" (Ezekiel 48:35—the final sentence of this whole description and the entire book). Ezekiel is not describing an earthly temple, but a future day when the Lord himself will be the High Priest (as a human high priest is not mentioned in these chapters). Also, if this temple were to have been constructed as described in chapter 48, it would be placed outside the city of Jerusalem—and this would make no sense. The tone of this author, again, is vitally important in understanding this prophet's message.[20]

Ultimately, Jewish scholars, led by Rabbi Hananyah ben Hezekiah, stated that there is no deviation from Mosaic laws as Ezekiel employed allegory rather than provided literal prescription for future worship in the millennium.[21] The ample evidence of the canonicity of Ezekiel made this minor debate short-lived.[22] Most compelling is that this book belongs in the category of the Prophets, the canonicity of which was closed by the first century AD.[23] Still, a closer examination of Ezekiel once again reveals the intense scrutiny that each book has undergone to secure its place in the Old Testament canon.

FALLING IN LOVE

Some of these Antilegomena books were meant to be read out loud, while one was written in captivity to provide hope for the hopeless. And the variances show that God is one of relationship rather than rules. In *Misreading Scripture with Western Eyes*, the authors, E. Randolph Richards and Brandon J. O'Brien, discuss Westerners' obsession of pigeonholing God to be a stickler for rules. They write, "It often seems as if God is sovereign over everything except his rules . . . [and Westerners] seem to insist upon God being bound to his own rules."

For example, a manager in a restaurant charges the same price for the meals set before the patrons and the menu states this clearly. But the authors explain, "Fees apply to everybody, unless the manager thinks someone really can't afford it. Then he makes an exception." They further explain, "Westerners might consider this arbitrary; many non-Western Christians consider this grace."[24] And indeed our God is one of immeasurable grace.

God did not write sixty-six books to reveal a robotic or despotic God so that people would conform to robotic or rule-following ways. Certainly there are rules—many, many rules. But because we could not fulfill them, Jesus did so perfectly for us. And because Jesus died the death we deserve, he now offers us life. He *is* the Life, and he invites us into a new way of living that's based on truth (John 14:6). We cannot live the lives that he intended for us apart from the Scriptures. And we cannot continue to listen to his rhythm or voice apart from the Scriptures. To stop reading the Scriptures would be like turning off the music—no beat, no lyrics, no harmony.

If the books of the Bible could be analogized to a music album, then we can say that not all of the songs have the same rhythm, message, or purpose. That would be boring, senseless, and a waste of space. Could you imagine picking up your favorite artist's next album and finding that all the songs had the same melody? We might ask for a refund.

God, who is the master Storyteller and Maestro, used different genres of writing to stir our hearts to love—because he loves us madly! The stars in the sky, the gorgeous sunset, the rain that drenches our land and souls. They are presented to us with loving, nail-scarred hands that never cease to reach out to hold ours. In this journey of life, God knows that we need hands to hold. And he offers his so that he can lovingly, reassuringly, and capably guide us from glory to glory and ultimately to home.

If we read the Scriptures like a life manual, it will fail to make sense. It would be like learning to dance by reading a dance manual. There are step-by-step guidebooks for various dances, but we all know that there's nothing like actually being led by a dance instructor on the dance floor. Though the Scriptures seem like only a book (and often mistaken for a guidebook), it is actually the Lord presenting himself to us. As we read these pages, my prayer is that we would dance with the Lord—absorbing, meditating, responding, and living out his love by the power of the Spirit.

Brian and I often end a long day with a dance of sorts. We call it the "penguin walk," where he holds me super close. I put both my feet on top of his feet, and he walks me around the living room. Sometimes we talk, many times we don't. It's one of my favorite ways to end the day.

I often feel as if I'm on a penguin walk with the Lord when I'm in the Scriptures. He holds me super close, and his words of love wrap around my soul. I cast my cares on him as he reminds me that he'll never leave me nor forsake me. Even though sometimes I feel like we're dancing in the dark, I'm okay because the darkness is not dark to God. Psalm 139:12 reminds me that darkness is as light with God.

After making the second confession, I still ask the Lord, "Please help me to understand your Word." But it's coupled with another request: "Please help me to love your Word." Asking for the ability to love seems unromantic in our culture, but I think it's one of the most romantic (and heroic) things we can do. Sometimes my love for Brian fails, and the emotions run dry and my actions fall short. But that's when I'll ask the Lord for a fresh dose of love for my husband because I know that true love's reservoir flows from God's heart and not mine. As we end this chapter, I pray that we would ask God anew for a love of the Scriptures. And in response, may we know that the Lord reaches out his hands right now and invites us to dance.

QUESTIONS TO PONDER

1. Which song most reminds you of God's love and faithfulness?

2. Which of the four books mentioned in this chapter makes more sense after proper categorization according to the Hebrew Bible? How so?

7

The Old Testament Fakes

HAVE YOU EVER come across counterfeit money or a knockoff designer item? From deep fakes to fake news, sometimes it's hard to tell what's real and what's fake. Sometimes it's easy to tell and it makes us cringe, but that's beside the point. If we're honest, fakes can be tempting. Fabricated joy, instantaneous faith, and love without effort don't sound bad sometimes. I have to check myself often because I'm tempted to veer toward fast, easy, and self-serving—all ingredients to fake Christianity. And the longer I walk with the Lord, the more I need to vigilantly guard my faith from these attitudes seeping in.

False Christianity can take many forms, but one of the most dangerous is to believe that we can know God apart from the Scriptures. There are many ways to experience God, but only one way to know his thoughts—and that's through his Word. Only his Word can cut to the quick and bring crystal-clear clarity to the complicated areas of life. There are many ways that God makes his presence known—a hug from a friend, a smile from a stranger, unexpected provision, much-needed healing. But without the Word, these gifts are murky translators to the mindset, heartbeat, and sacrificial love of the Giver.

Many questions in life leave us confused, feeling directionless and stuck. Sometimes confusion settles in through less serious means. When *The Da Vinci Code* was released in 2003, I could not put down Dan Brown's novel. After I consumed it ravenously, I momentarily wondered, *What if Jesus did have a child with Mary Magdalene?* (This is the premise of the book for those who don't know the storyline.) I knew the proposition was preposterous from a Judeo-Christian standpoint, but I realized then that I had very little historical and biblical knowledge to refute its claim.[1]

Somewhere in my heart I knew that Jesus was who he claimed to be in the four Gospels. If he did have a wife, it would have been written in the Gospels. But moments like this exposed the fragility of my beliefs because I had yet to fully embrace the Scriptures as the very Word of God.

For Protestants, we believe that the sixty-six books of the Bible are from God—and we also believe that this is a closed canon. This means that no other book that has ever been written or ever will be written can be added to this list of sixty-six. All other works, however inspiring, are not *inspired*. The God-breathed words that 2 Timothy 3:16 refers to only applies to these books and to none other.[2]

But how do we arrive at this conclusion? We can easily eschew *The Da Vinci Code* because it's fictitious, but how about extrabiblical works regarded by some as holy texts from God? If someone tried to pay for groceries with counterfeit money, the rational thing would be to assess the currency. In the same way, our investigation of the Scriptures should include a close-up look at the counterfeits. But some counterfeits are harder to discern than others. Some clearly look like Monopoly money, but others are uncannily similar to the original.

Bible-believing Protestant Christians generally call these books *apocryphal*, but not all apocryphal books hold the same weight. The many canonical lists and shifting terminologies applied to the books therein can be complicated—there are many books dedicated just to listing the lists![3] For our purposes, we'll include those considered to be principal inclusions in pseudepigraphal (extrabiblical) lists as well as the apocryphal works that have generated more debates.

PSEUDEPIGRAPHA

Unlike the books in the Homologoumena and Antilegomena, those in the Pseudepigrapha (meaning "false writings") were considered "nonbiblical works" and "spurious religious writings" within the ancient Jewish community from the outset. There are many books in this category, but the list below is considered the standard collection.

Legendary

* The Book of Jubilee

* The Letter of Aristeas

* The Book of Adam and Eve

* The Martyrdom of Isaiah

Apocalyptic

* 1 Enoch

* The Testament of the Twelve Patriarchs

* The Sibylline Oracle

* The Assumption of Moses

* 2 Enoch, or the Book of the Secrets of Enoch

* 2 Baruch, or The Syriac Apocalypse of Baruch

* 3 Baruch, or The Greek Apocalypse of Baruch

Didactic

* 3 Maccabees

* 4 Maccabees

* Pirke Aboth

* The Story of Ahikar

Poetical

* The Psalms of Solomon

* Psalm 151

Historical

* The Fragment of a Zadokite Work[4]

None of these books' historical or religious contributions should be discounted, but more importantly, these books were deemed pseudepigraphal for rightful reasons. Some, for example the Letter of Aristeas, are pseudonymous, meaning they were purposefully written under a fictitious name. Such books never vied for canonical status, nor was the honor given to them.[5] Some are from origins other than what they claim.[6] Also, some of these books are not all false in content. For example, Jude 9, 14-15 refer to the Book of Enoch and the Assumption of Moses; and 2 Timothy 3:8 seems to refer to the *Penitence of Jannes and Jambres*.[7] We should keep in mind, though, that Paul quoted from non-Christian poets such as Aratus, Menander, and Epimenides (Acts 17:28; 1 Corinthians 15:33; Titus 1:12). Bible scholars remind us that "Truth is truth no matter where it is found, whether it is uttered by a heathen poet, a pagan prophet (Numbers 24:15-16), a dumb animal (Numbers 22:28), or even a demon (Acts 16:17)."[8]

The scriptural mention of literature outside of Scripture doesn't make it Scripture. In other words, just because Scripture includes snippets from non-scriptural sources, it does not elevate the original non-scriptural source to scriptural status. One telltale sign that Scripture is referencing other parts of Scripture is when terminology such as "it is written" or "the Scripture says" prefaces the insertion. No part of the Pseudepigrapha has ever been attached with such an introduction in Scripture.

INTERTESTAMENTAL PERIOD

One pertinent fact is timing. A majority of these noncanonical works were written in what is known as the intertestamental period. This is the period between the writings of the Old and New Testaments, hence the term *intertestamental* ("between the testaments"). The four centuries prior to Christ's birth are sometimes known as "the four hundred silent years" because there is a gap in biblical records.[9] Christians sometimes refer to this time as a period of God's silence. This means that the newest addition to the Hebrew Old Testament was written approximately four hundred years before the birth of Christ, and a bulk of the writing predates the incarnation by a much longer span of time.[10]

Once again, reverse chronological order is helpful. Starting with the birth of Christ, let's go back four hundred years to examine the intertestamental period. At the start of this period, the Persian Empire ruled a vast stretch of land, including where the Israelites lived. The Persians, however, were soon conquered by Alexander the Great who overtook this region. He secured his dominance through victories over the Persians at the battles of Granicus (334 BC), Issus (333 BC), and Arbela (331 BC, the same year that he founded Alexandria in Egypt).[11]

Hailing from Greece-Macedonia, Alexander brought Greek culture with him and started Hellenizing this whole region. It's not a surprise that the Old Testament was translated into Greek during this time—resulting in the Septuagint. The significance and development of the Septuagint are rooted in this timespan and location.[12]

The making of the Septuagint, also called LXX (seventy in roman numerals), is steeped in both mystery and legend. Supposedly seventy elders (or seventy-two elders, six from each tribe of Israel) were tasked by King Ptolemy to translate the Old Testament from Hebrew into Greek. Allegedly these elders were placed in seventy-two separate rooms for seventy-two days but somehow miraculously created seventy-two exact replicas of one another. This is largely a fabrication. King Ptolemy did invite Jewish elders to commit to this work of translation, but they only translated the Pentateuch and most likely in collaboration with one another. The rest of the Old Testament was translated by other Jewish scholars. The complete translation of the Old Testament from Hebrew to Greek was completed by c. 250–150 BC.[13]

The LXX (used interchangeably with *Septuagint* going forward) is more than another bit of information, albeit a significant one, in church history. The LXX is like a magic key for Christians and deserves special attention. Those seeking to better understand the canon will be empowered by understanding the Septuagint's development and usage—because through the Septuagint both illumination *and confusion* set in among the Jews. The Greek-speaking Jews revered the Septuagint as the holy Scriptures, but confusion set in during the second century BC. Once the entire Hebrew Old Testament was translated into Greek, various Jewish scribes *added* additional books to the LXX that were never a part of the Hebrew canon. These books are commonly known as the "Apocrypha"[14] or "deuterocanonical" books, deriving from the Greek word *deuteros* which means "second."[15] The term *deuterocanonical* rightly implies that these books were not primary in their inclusion of the Hebrew Bible.

It would be like today's Bibles that contain commentaries or appendixes. But in our highly literate world, there are clear delineations that demarcate the prologue, main body, epilogue, and so on. In the predominately oral tradition and societies of the ancient Near East, such demarcation was largely unknown. Hence, subsequent generations came to fuse them into the Hebrew Old Testament canon, and this caused confusion for the Jewish communities in the Greek-speaking regions and among the early church fathers.

THE OLD TESTAMENT APOCRYPHA

Books considered pseudepigraphal were clearly noncanonical within Jewish tradition, but those labeled as apocryphal created more confusion. For example, the Roman Catholic Church includes all sixty-six books of the Protestant Bible but adds additional books to their canon; and the Eastern Orthodox groups include even more books than the Catholics.[16] Not only are the apocryphal books themselves numerous, so are the canonical lists. Each category of lists (for example, the Greek Christian List and Latin Christian List) have many variations, depending on who compiled the lists.[17] Many of these lists derive from the LXX, which included the Hebrew Bible *and* appended books that are now deemed apocryphal.

Now, this is when things get really interesting. Once again, the timing of the LXX is exceptionally important. The LXX was written c. 250–150 BC.[18] Besides the Septuagint, other Jewish writings appeared during the intertestamental period. Perhaps some of these titles are familiar: 1 and 2 Maccabees, The Letter of Jeremiah, and Bel and the Dragon. These are just three of the fourteen or fifteen books (depending on categorization) considered a part of the Old Testament Apocrypha. *Apocrypha* means "hidden" as in mysterious, or "hidden" as in cast aside because they have no real value. These are the principal Old Testament Apocryphal books in chronological order:

1. The Letter of Jeremiah (c. 300–100 BC)

2. Tobit (c. 200 BC)

3. Judith (c. 150 BC)

4. 1 Esdras (c. 150–100 BC)

5. Baruch (c. 150–50 BC)

6. Additions to Esther (140–130 BC)

7. 1 Maccabees (c. 110 BC)

8. 2 Maccabees (c. 110-70 BC)

9. Prayer of Azariah (second or first century BC) (Song of Three Young Men)

10. Prayer of Manasseh (second or first century BC)

11. Susanna (second or first century BC)

12. Ecclesiasticus (Sirach) (132 BC)

13. Bel and the Dragon (c. 100 BC)

14. Wisdom of Solomon (c. 30 BC)

15. 2 Esdras (c. AD 100)[19]

All of the Old Testament Apocryphal books were written during the intertestamental period with the exception of 2 Esdras (c. AD 100); they were written mostly after 200 BC, and Jewish tradition notes that God closed the Old Testament canon around 400 BC. The Talmud records that "the Holy Spirit departed from Israel" after "the latter prophets Haggai, Zechariah . . . and Malachi," with the writing of Malachi, which dates to c. 450 BC.[20] This means that about two hundred years passed before the Old Testament Apocryphal books started to appear after the Hebrew canon was closed.

Two hundred years of silence can be deafening. No word through a prophet, no miracles recorded, and no visions or dreams. Waiting in a period of silence can make people do interesting things. Let's be honest, people from all cultures and time periods just aren't good at waiting. I'm not only talking about twenty-first-century moderns who expect immediate text replies and search furtively for the shortest checkout lines. Impatience is a timeless human condition. Think about the golden calf that Aaron and the Israelites made when Moses "delayed to come down from the mountain [Sinai]," when he received the Ten Commandments from God (Exodus 32). Or when Saul made the unlawful sacrifice after "he waited seven days, the time set by Samuel; but Samuel did not come" (1 Samuel 13:8-9). Both show a deep desire for spiritual things—except it's not according to God's timetable or God's dictates.

In many ways, the Israelites, too, were craving spiritual enlightenment during the intertestamental period. They were living under foreign rulers and awaiting their Messiah. It is not a surprise that counterfeits to the Bible would be created at such a time. Also, the Apocrypha was never given official canonicity status

until the Council of Trent, which took place between AD 1545–
1563. That's the sixteenth century *anno Domini*—which is the
passage of well over a *thousand* years. Even non-historians would
pause at this wide gap in time and ask, "Why so late?" The Roman
Catholic Church proclaimed the Apocrypha as canonical during
the Protestant Reformation, a time rife with tension, and this was
a political move of sorts. When Martin Luther nailed his Ninety-
Five Theses on the doors of Wittenberg in 1517, the Catholic
Church needed to substantiate and justify their doctrines against
Protestant ones. The timing of both the creation and canonization
of the Apocrypha should be duly noted.

Unlike golden calves or unlawful sacrifices, however, the Apocrypha is not profane, at least not all of it. There are many good
messages, and some parts reflect New Testament ideals. For example, Matthew 7:16 states, "By their fruit you will recognize
them"; and Sirach 27:6 declares, "The fruit of a tree declares the
husbandry thereof." But then many passages contradict the Protestant Bible, such as those that encourage prayers for the dead
(2 Maccabees 12:45 states, "He made the atoning sacrifice for
those who had died, that they might be released from their sin")
and salvation by works (Tobit 12:9 states, "Alms delivers from
death, and it purges away all sin. Those who give alms and do
righteousness will be filled with life").

Despite the theological claims that contradict the Hebrew Old
Testament, the Apocrypha was given credibility by Jewish leaders
during the intertestamental period as useful documents in religious instruction. Hence, the Apocrypha was appended to the
Septuagint, which came to be known as the "Alexandrian list."[21]
This list compiled in Alexandria included the Hebrew Old Testament *and* the Apocrypha. The Jewish people during this time,

however, never accepted the Apocrypha as canonical, and this is important to reiterate. They were, in this time of silence, yearning for spiritual enlightenment and found edification in these works, but never claimed them to be Scripture. Confusion set in when some church fathers misunderstood the Hebrew tradition and regarded some apocryphal books as canonical. That part of our history will be examined in chapters twelve and thirteen.

ONLY TWO CHOICES

In every era, we have the choice between accepting Scripture or not. There are true Scriptures, and there are false ones. When confronted with the Bible, we either hold to its truth or fall away from it. And Charles Templeton and Billy Graham epitomize these diverging paths. These men were once preaching partners and close friends, but their friendship drifted as each chose a different course. The world knows of Graham, but what about Templeton? He was born in Toronto in 1915, became a "born-again Christian" in 1936, preached (often alongside Graham) to crowded stadiums throughout the 1950s, resigned from ministry in 1957, entered thereafter into a variety of professions (including writing), and died in 2001 after battling Alzheimer's disease.[22] His eventful life is noted for many things and for many achievements, but perhaps his denial of the Christian faith is the most notable. Templeton's crisis of faith eventually led him to renounce the Christian belief, and his book *Farewell to God* says it all. How does a noted evangelist become a self-professed agnostic? By discounting the Word of God.

Billy Graham notes that Templeton started "undergoing serious theological difficulties, particularly concerning the authority of the Scriptures" in 1948–1949. And in the summer of 1949,

Templeton told Graham, "Billy, you're fifty years out of date. People no longer accept the Bible as being inspired the way you do. Your faith is too simple."[23] Then, Templeton relays in his own words an important conversation between the two:

> Templeton: "But, Billy, it's simply not possible any longer to believe, for instance, the biblical account of creation."

> Graham: "I believe in the Genesis account of creation because it's in the Bible. I've discovered something in my ministry: when I take the Bible literally, when I proclaim it as the Word of God, my preaching has power. . . . I don't have the time or the intellect to examine all sides of each theological dispute, so I've decided, once and for all, to stop questioning and accept the Bible as God's Word."

> Templeton: "But, Billy . . . you can't do that. You don't dare stop thinking about the most important question in life. Do it and you begin to die. It's intellectual suicide."

> Graham: "I don't know about anybody else, but I've decided that that's the path for me."[24]

Two men. Two different paths. One lived a faithful life built on the Scriptures. The other, after rejecting the Scriptures as God's Word, spent his life searching for meaning but never seemed to find it.

At the end of Templeton's life, he met with journalist Lee Strobel and graciously consented to give an interview though he was suffering from Alzheimer's. Strobel asked, "And so how do you assess this Jesus?" And Templeton replied, "He was the greatest human being who has ever lived. . . . He was the intrinsically wisest person I've ever encountered in my life or in my readings."

Strobel was surprised by this response and followed up with, "You sound like you really care about him." And Templeton said, 'Well, yes, he's the most important thing in my life . . . I . . . I . . . I know it may sound strange, but I have to say . . . I *adore* him! . . . I . . . miss . . . him!" Templeton's voice began to crack toward the end of that last statement, and he wept.[25]

How the rest of Templeton's life unfolded, especially the inner workings of his heart and mind, only God knows. But we are certain that our God loves and pursues until the very last breath. And what we know is that life apart from the Scriptures leads to confusion and futility.

This is true not only for Templeton, but for Billy Graham as well. Graham was afflicted with angst and turmoil until he wholeheartedly accepted the Bible as God's Word. Billy Graham traveled the globe, counseled many American presidents, and spoke to millions on one authority alone—the authority of the Scriptures.

There might be seasons where the opposite seems true, that life can be fulfilling and meaningful apart from accepting the Bible as God's Word—but those seasons are short-lived. Children move out, jobs change, our bodies grow weak, the other political party gets elected, stocks plummet, friends move far away or ghost us, or divorce papers are served. Only God's Word can provide the unshifting, true, and life-giving counsel that we need through every season in life's journey.

Our eternal lives depend on the first confession (accepting Jesus as Lord and Savior), but the substance and integrity of our earthly lives depend on making the second confession. Without a wholehearted embrace of the Scriptures, we will be like sojourners lost in the dark. No light, no direction, no hope.

There might be ideas and theologies that contradict the God of the Bible. Let's tackle those headlong. Let's do due diligence, get educated, be aware. But when discerning counterfeit money, the best thing to do is to compare it, side-by-side, with the original. For every competing doctrine (or literal or proverbial pseudepigraphic or apocryphal work), let's immerse ourselves in a double portion of Scripture and let God's Word bring light and life into our minds and souls.

QUESTIONS TO PONDER

1. Are you currently waiting on God for an answer or breakthrough? If so, how do you think God wants you to spend this time of waiting?

2. How do Graham and Templeton's lives reveal the pivotal role that Scripture can take when we face doubts and trials in our lives?

8

Miracles

ONE OF MY FAVORITE C. S. LEWIS ANALOGIES comes from *Surprised by Joy*. Before the Oxford don became a follower of Jesus, he mused that if God should exist, the matter would be irrelevant to him. Just like Hamlet (a created being) could never know Shakespeare (the creator), there was no way that man could know God; and there was "no possibility of being in a personal relation with Him."[1]

This thought came to Lewis during a pivotal season of his life, when he transitioned from atheism to Christianity. Lewis, ever the intellect, likened his interchange with God as a game of chess. And God, in 1929, masterfully moved toward "checkmate." One way that God "began to make His final moves" was by sending Christian friends, such as H. V. D. Dyson and J. R. R. Tolkien. Of the latter, Lewis writes that he befriended him despite serious warnings never to trust a papist or a philologist, and "Tolkien was both."[2]

God further advanced on the chessboard by walking Lewis through his own thoughts. He revealed to Lewis the full logic of his analogy, making him realize that Hamlet could indeed know Shakespeare, if Shakespeare would write himself into the play and introduce himself to Hamlet. Further, "The 'Shakespeare' within the play would of course be at once Shakespeare and one of Shakespeare's creatures. It would bear some analogy to Incarnation."[3]

My eyes widened and jaw dropped the first time I heard this brilliant analogy. *Of course*, I thought, *God wrote himself into the play of humanity in the form of Jesus, who is God himself.* Jesus became man so he could personally relate to us. In doing so he demonstrated that the miraculous and mundane, the virgin birth of a baby born in a manger, intersect in the story of God.

The incarnation was a miracle, the Bible is full of miracles, and God still works miracles today. Biblical scholar Craig Keener states that the most common definition of *miracle*, "from Augustine to Aquinas, has been a divine action that transcends the ordinary course of nature and so generates awe." Unlike "unusually awesome sunsets," this awe stems from "something you would never expect to happen on its own."[4]

Miracles are all around us, as they have been since the dawn of time. But the Enlightenment and post-Enlightenment philosophies have embedded, especially in the western world, a "thoroughgoing suspicion of all supernatural claims." Keener's two-volume work on miracles traces their occurrences all around the world, including Asia, Africa, Latin America, and the Caribbean.[5] When looking at miracles in a global context experienced by tens of millions of people, it is impossible to dismiss these supernatural events as mere coincidences.[6]

Before transitioning to the New Testament, this chapter is meant to take a step back to assess the reasonableness of faith. And faith is nothing short of miraculous. There are those who have witnessed radical healings—people bound to wheelchairs who are able to walk, and near-death patients who come instantaneously to full health.[7] But there is a different kind of miraculous that is less visible but no less astounding—and that's the miracle of faith. Keener writes, "Whether we label it a 'miracle' or not, it is divine action that makes possible a relationship with God."[8] Both types of miracles, both external and internal, are intrinsic to Scripture. Wherever we might be on our faith journey, may the Scriptures illuminate our path so we don't miss the moments when the miraculous converges with the ordinary.

MIRACLES IN THE SCRIPTURES

To believe *in* the Scriptures is a miracle: to believe the central claim of the Bible—that fallen humanity's Savior is none other than Jesus—is a true miracle. It is no less miraculous than a dead person coming back to life. Keener, one of the leading scholars on miracles, writes that his own salvation moment was no less miraculous than any public miracle he has recounted.

A big part of the miraculous work of salvation centers on the people whom God sends. Sometimes God sends the likes of Tolkien and Dyson. Other times, he sends devout relatives. The latter was true of Keener, who tells of his Methodist relatives who prayed faithfully for him and his family for years. Their prayers seemed to have worked as Keener slowly segued from atheism to agnosticism.

During this season, Keener found himself in a forty-five-minute debate with conservative Baptist street preachers dressed in black suits. He demanded of them, "If there's a God, where did the dinosaur bones come from?" Keener admits that the question was "logically fallacious—why should the existence of God conflict with the existence of dinosaurs?—but neither I nor (apparently) they yet understood that point."

Keener continues, "On the spot and having to come up with a quick answer, one retorted, 'The devil put them there.' Disgusted,

I walked away." But within the next hour or two he experienced a profound miracle. He experienced God more tangibly than "another person physically talking" to him in the same room. And he was "overwhelmed with God's own presence." Everything that the Baptist street preachers professed—about the Bible asserting we must be "made right with God"—suddenly became a reality to Keener. He notes, "I actually felt God come inside me."[9]

Just as the street preachers probably did not imagine such a radical conversion experience just hours after their exchange about dinosaur bones, God can do miracles beyond our expectations. We don't have to be Oxford dons, devout prayer warriors, or know anything about paleontology to be used by God. He can use any of us, and many times we might not know what seeds we are sowing when we proclaim the truth of the Scriptures.

When I came to faith at seventeen, I was the only Christian in my family. Although I was afraid, I shared my faith with both my parents and my two siblings. My sister, Jennifer, in particular, was initially very hostile toward Christianity. And at one point she said, "If you ever bring up Christianity again, I'm never going to talk to you." I knew her to be a woman of her word, so I was a little desperate and fumbled for words. In response I said, "Um okay, I won't bring it up again, but can I say one last thing? If one day I disappear and lots of other people are gone [I was thinking of the rapture], and someone asks you to take a mark on your forehead, don't do it." I think this answer was worse than the dinosaur-bone response, but I was only a teenager and had been reading too much on end times. She rolled her eyes and walked away, probably as disgusted as Keener.

But within a couple of months, God's light entered into her heart and she came to faith. Since then she's built her life on the truth of the Scriptures, as have my parents and brother. They each have a beautiful relationship with the Lord, and watching each of their faith journeys has been nothing short of witnessing four miracles.

I'm still waiting on some miracles though. I have loved ones who still haven't accepted Jesus' invitation of salvation and eternal life. Our dear friends who introduced us to a new world of camping are high on that list. So are my neighbors who throw the best parties and offer the warmest hospitality. And I'm reminded that my fumbling and lack of winsome words never stopped God from using me. I know the same is true for any other follower willing to share the truth of the Scriptures as best they know how.

Perhaps there is a person in your life who has yet to come to faith, and you feel discouraged by their lack of interest toward God or their animosity toward Christianity. I hope that Lewis's and Keener's stories, and perhaps mine, will encourage you to press on. Let's seek opportunities to show love through words and deed, and perhaps through avenues like camping and parties. Let's continue to pray for our loved ones to come to faith, knowing that our God is a God of miracles.

MIRACLES THROUGHOUT THE SCRIPTURES

The many miracles throughout Scripture have sometimes deterred seekers from taking the Bible seriously. Healings, walking on water, and the dead coming back to life might dissuade realists from embracing the Bible. But C. S. Lewis wrote that "I have never found any philosophical grounds for the universal negative proposition that miracles do not happen."[10] Lewis has much more to say on the topic, and his book, appropriately titled *Miracles*, goes into much detail. In it he defines the miraculous as "an interference with Nature by supernatural power."[11] It takes a certain type of faith to disbelieve miracles as much as it takes faith to believe in them. Just because someone hasn't witnessed or experienced a miracle doesn't mean that miracles don't exist.

Joy Davidson, C. S. Lewis's wife, also weighed in on this topic as she wielded the pen mightily in her own right. She was a gifted poet and writer who captivated Lewis's heart, and Davidson's writings also captivate audiences today. Her recollection of her journey with the Scriptures is especially poignant.

Davidson notes that she initially read the Bible as a great work of fiction. But soon she started asking herself, "Could this be a report of fact?" This question arose from "incongruities," which "proved rather than disproved the veracity of scripture." Davidson wrote, "Fiction is always congruous, life usually incongruous. In fiction there is a unity of effect, of style; the people all say exactly what they should say to be in character and in the mood." But not the Bible. For example, Davidson notes that the apostles would "never have told so many stories which made them look silly."[12]

Davidson ultimately came to faith in Jesus as she "could not doubt the divinity of Jesus [that] followed logically [from] orthodox Christian theology." She notes, "My modernist objections to the miraculous proved to be mere superstition, unsupported by logic. I am a writer of fiction; I have made up stories myself, and I think I can tell a made-up story from a true one. The men who told of the resurrection told of something they had *seen*. Not Shakespeare himself could have invented the Synoptic Gospels."[13]

Both Davidson and Lewis note the power and limit of human words, and how they point to but pale in comparison to the Word. The incarnate God came as man and gifted us the Word to tell this incredible tale filled with miracles and new life. Not even

Shakespeare or the greatest writers can make up the story of redemption. The miracles throughout Scripture do not invalidate God's truth, but, rather, substantiate it.

Interestingly, Jesus performed many miracles while on earth, but he never reveled in them. In fact, Jesus resisted miracles "on demand," despite opportunities to exert his might.[14] His first miracle, at the wedding at Cana, was at the urging of his mother. Jesus also refused to perform a miracle during his last moment on earth, as he hung on the cross and was incited to perform one to save himself. Throughout his life, whether before Herod or Satan in the wilderness, Jesus refused to allow his powers to be manipulated, despite provocations and taunts to perform miracles. When Jesus did heal, it was at his will and prompted by his love. Each touch, each healing was never an end to itself but pointed to the heart of the Savior. The love that compelled the miracles of Jesus is the same love that pursues us today.

MIRACLE OF THE SCRIPTURES

Just like the virgin birth is a miracle, the birth of Scripture, the birthing of "the oracles of God," is equally miraculous.[15] But it takes faith to believe it as such. Unlike those who disbelieve the Scriptures *because* of the miraculous claims, there are those who discount God's Word because it seems too base. Lewis notes that the Word of God can seem like an "untidy and leaky vehicle" when we would have preferred "an unrefracted light giving us ultimate truth in systematic form—something we could have tabulated and memorized and relied on like the multiplication table." Instead, as Lewis observes, the Word, especially Jesus' words, includes "paradox, proverb, exaggeration, parable, irony; even (I mean no irreverence) the 'wisecrack.'"[16] And there can be many questions that linger in our minds as to the canon, such as the books in the Antilegomena and Apocrypha.

This is when another comparison with the Word of God and the Son of God is helpful. After all, Jesus claimed to be fulfillment of the Law and Prophets (Matthew 5:17). Christians might want to place the "unrefracted" light on the birth of Christ, and our Christmas pageants and celebrations certainly try. And no doubt the Christmas story is beautiful, but it's also *absurd* (I mean no irreverence, to borrow Lewis's words).[17]

The familiarity of Jesus' birth shouldn't deter us from seeing the wonderfully absurd: God impregnated a teenage girl from a humble family, the Savior was birthed in a manger, his parents lost him when he was twelve years old, his family worried about his mental health, and so much more *human* stuff. Also, Jesus did not look the part of a Savior; he wasn't the military or political leader that the Jews were awaiting, and he "had no beauty or majesty to attract us to him, nothing in his appearance that we should desire him" (Isaiah 53:2). Yet, God dovetails the miraculous with the mundane, and we, as Christians, believe it all.

God used very human means to create the Word as well, and it might not seem perfect from our viewpoint. Lewis writes, "I cannot be the only reader who has wondered why God, having given [the apostle Paul] so many gifts, withheld from him (what would to us seem so necessary for the first Christian theologian) that of lucidity and orderly expression."[18] Touché, Lewis. There have been times, to be honest, when I wonder if the translation or the original wording make some of the Epistles read like long, run-on sentences.

Lewis observes that "the human qualities of the raw materials" peek out, as "naïveté, error, contradiction, even (as in the cursing psalms) wickedness are not removed."[19] Despite what might not make human sense, Lewis notes that "God must have done what is best, this is best, therefore God has done this." In the important work of writing and canonizing Scripture, there is a "Divine pressure" in all.[20]

God does as he wishes, and he is tied to no higher authority. Yet, the methods he chose might not make sense to us. After the birth of Jesus, Herod, in a rage, ordered the killing of all Jewish boys two and under in and near Bethlehem (Matthew 2:16-18, Jeremiah 31:15). It makes no human sense that the birth of the world's Savior would be accompanied with the slaughter of innocent babies. Yet, that's a part of the Christian story. Even the confusing and nonlinear parts of the story are a part of our heritage.

The story of canonization, too, can seem too *human* or too *base* to be called divine. But if we are familiar with the methods of our God, the history of canonization should not surprise us. Our God often uses lowly and ordinary means to reveal himself. Ordinary equipment, like parchment and ink, and human means, like scribes and councils, were undoubtedly guided by our loving God to give us the living Word. The God who traversed time and space to enter into humanity, desires to keep the channels of communication open. The Holy Spirit continues to speak to us through the Word so that we can hear the voice of the Good Shepherd. The journey of life can be hard to navigate, and God's Word promises to guide us through every twist and turn. I know that I have a tendency to veer off the right path, get lost and distracted, and find myself in a dark place occasionally. But I'm so thankful that the Scriptures shine light and bring me back to safety every time I ask.

MIRACLES THROUGH THE SCRIPTURES

Have you ever experienced a miracle *through* God's Word? There have been pivotal seasons of my life where I needed a miracle, and nothing else would do. Indeed, the miracle came—and it often came through the Scriptures. One particular moment comes to mind to illustrate this point. Our son, JD, was born at twenty-four and a half weeks, weighing less than two pounds. His life was touch-and-go for the first months, and each day was lived on pins and needles. He often turned blue (literally blue) while feeding because his lungs were still underdeveloped. And when his cardiologist wheeled him into surgery a couple of weeks after birth, I discovered for the first time why people say they feel weak in the knees. I literally could not stand up because I was so anxious and worried.

I still remember where I was sitting during the surgery, next to the window and facing a big clock. During the surgery I took out my Bible and read the next chapter of my devotional. I was in 2 Kings 4, and I read about how Elisha raised the Shunammite woman's son from the dead. And when I got to verse thirty-six and read "Take up your son," I literally felt this resurrection power surge through those words, as if God was speaking them to me about JD. It was surreal. As I was reading those words, I stood up to meet the surgeon who at that moment walked into the waiting room and said, "The surgery was textbook. He's doing great."

That was a huge milestone, but JD was not out of the woods yet. He stayed in the NICU for ninety-seven days, and then came home with an oxygen tank about my height. The next seven years were filled with more doctors' visits and emergency room visits than I can count. Brian and I still talk about how we aged at a rapid rate during that time. For me, those were long and arduous years of exhaustion and sometimes confusion. But God's Word,

"Take up your son," resounded in my soul, replenishing hope and renewing my strength over and over.

That experience taught me to stay consistent in my Bible reading. Many times the next reading was not nearly as eventful as this one. But consistent reading of the Word always yields benefits, even if they don't surface for years. And even when the Word is not miraculously experienced, it's still working wonders.

QUESTIONS TO PONDER

1. Have you ever encountered a miracle? If so, what do you think God was trying to convey in this miracle?

2. What can you change in your schedule this week to consume more of God's Word?

9

A Close-Up of the New Testament

MOST BOOKS ON the canon include a discussion of the word *testament* early on, but I've purposefully saved this word for now. Words matter, and I want to introduce this word at a pinpointed junction in our discussion. When and how a word is said can make all the difference. In our day and age, we are fast learning that even a singular word, whether spoken or tweeted, can have far-reaching effects. Words can both confuse and clarify. And *testament* has done both. As we shift our study from the Old to the New Testament, this is prime time to think about the larger categorization of the Bible into the Old and New Testaments.

Testament is often correlated to a "last will and testament." The Latin *testamentum* from which we get our word *testament* mostly means a settlement or agreement. The Latin term is derived from the Greek word *diathēkē*, which can refer to a will but is more commonly associated with a contract between people of unequal status.[1] *Diathēkē* is better translated as "covenant" and more fully describes our bond with God.

Testament has a ring of something legal only. Recently Brian had to slog through a long contract before signing it, and I was especially glad that both of my siblings are lawyers; the legalese was hard to understand. Perhaps sometimes we think of the Old and New Testaments as just that—a legal document that's very hard to understand. There are rules in there that we mustn't break— and if we do, God can rain down curses or abandon us. There are rules that if we follow, we are given healthy bodies, extra money to spend, and good friends. If we see the Bible as a two-part testament that binds us in a legal contract with God (who vigilantly watches if we break any rules), the Scriptures might feel like chains squeezing out the joy and freedom in life.

Covenant has an entirely different ring to it. The best analogy would be a marriage contract. Brian and I have a marriage license and that means we're legally bound in so many ways, but the legalities are secondary to my relationship with him. Love, trust, enjoyment, and fun are a few things that take precedence over (and substantiate) our marriage contract. I don't remember the last time I looked at our marriage license, but I do remember our last date night. The legal implications might be the same for a contract and covenant, but the former usually does not require a bonding of the heart, while the latter does.

That's why a marriage covenant might most closely resemble the sacred and binding union behind the word *covenant*. Unlike human marriages that are (mostly) the union of equals, though, the eternal divide between a perfect God and fallen humanity is unequal in standing. In this covenant, as the original Greek denotes, the one with power offers privileges and treasures to those who could never acquire such things on their own. The unique nature of the word *covenant*, then, shows the unique relationship that God offers to his people, in love, provision, and protection.

THE NEW COVENANT

God initiates and issues a covenant with us today. It's a new covenant as described in the twenty-seven books of what we call the New Testament. They shed light on and surpass the old covenant described in the thirty-nine books of what we call the Old Testament. Hence, if we labeled the Bible as divided between the Old Covenant and the New Covenant, these terms would set clearer expectations of our relationship with God. From here on out, I will use the terms *testament* and *covenant* interchangeably, understanding that they refer to both the legal- and heart-bonding of the parties involved.

The first covenant in the Bible is known as the Noahic covenant in Genesis 9:8-17. This was where God promised never to destroy the earth again with flood, and he gave the rainbow as his sign of promise. There are three other examples of Old Testament covenants: the Abrahamic, Mosaic, and Davidic covenants[2]—and the Abrahamic also had an external sign, which was the circumcision of the foreskin. Collectively, the Old Covenant points to all the laws that the Israelites kept in order to be in harmony with God.

These Old Testament covenants are still meaningful to us today because Jesus is both the fulfillment and fulfiller of these covenants. Under the New Covenant, the people of God are no longer bound by a circumcision of the flesh but a circumcision of the heart. And this circumcision is not initiated or achieved by human obedience or religiosity, but it's fulfilled by Jesus. The Son of Man lived a sinless life, died a substitutionary death, and resurrected from the grave so that he can fulfill every last requirement under the Old Covenant. And by having faith in him, we become the beneficiaries of all the promises under the New Covenant.

These promises were written for us in twenty-seven different books, which started out as twenty-seven separate scrolls. These scrolls were written largely independently from one another, from approximately AD 45 (at the earliest) to about AD 100, and circulated separately from one another until about the second century. Also these twenty-seven scrolls were penned by nine human authors selected by God.[3] Following Jesus' resurrection, starting with the Epistles, these authors wrote about Jesus, about whom the whole Scriptures, both Old and New, testify.[4]

JESUS, A REAL HISTORICAL FIGURE

Before examining the books of the New Covenant, let's take a brief, albeit very important, moment to confirm the historicity of Jesus. Did Jesus of Nazareth even exist? The answer is a definitive yes. Even if you don't believe that the Bible is inspired, there is no denying the existence of Jesus of Nazareth as a historical figure.[5] Aside from the New Testament, there are reliable first- and second-century sources that substantiate the life of Jesus. Actually, *opponents* of the Christian faith serve as the most verifiable evidence of his existence and teachings.

Pliny (AD 61–113), who was the governor of Bithynia, serves as a prime example; his letters to Emperor Trajan (AD 53–117) provide a window into the Christ-following community in Bithynia. Trajan had sent Pliny to Bithynia in AD 110, which was a province south of the Black Sea. This was the Bithynia that Peter addressed in his first letter ("To God's elect, exiles scattered throughout the provinces of Pontus, Galatia, Cappadocia, Asia and Bithynia." 1 Peter 1:1). Some Roman leaders in the first and second centuries were upset by Christians, and Pliny wrote to Trajan complaining about these troublesome "Christians." Pliny noted that these Christians comprised "*many* of all ages and every rank and also of both sexes" that became a powerful, mass movement. Their numbers grew so exponentially that the pagan temples were largely deserted and business for animal sacrifices and other temple rituals were hit hard.[6] Pliny undoubtedly felt that the Christians were a nuisance since their practices negatively affected the Roman economy, among other ways that Christians failed to conform to Roman precepts. And these Christians were followers of none other than Jesus of Nazareth.

Tacitus (AD 55–120), Roman historian and governor of the province of Asia, provides more historical proof to Jesus' existence. He wrote in his *Annals of Imperial Rome* that Emperor Nero had tried to blame the Christians for the burning of Rome. In Tacitus's own words, he writes: "The conflagration was the result of an order . . . [and] Nero fastened the guilt . . . on a class hated for their abominations, called Christians by the populace." Further, Tacitus mentions Jesus in the same paragraph: "Christus, from whom the name had its origin, suffered the extreme penalty during the reign of Tiberius at the hand of one of our procurators, Pontius Pilate." Tiberius (42 BC–AD 37) was the emperor who ruled the Roman Empire during Jesus' death and resurrection,[7] and Pontius Pilate is known to most Christians because of his mention in the Gospels.

Roman historian Suetonius (AD 69–140) and Jewish historian Flavius Josephus (AD 37–100) also corroborate the existence of Jesus. In his *Life of Nero* (16.2), Suetonius condemned the Christians as a "class of man given to a new and wicked superstition." Suetonius's take on the Christian faith was not very favorable, which is not surprising given the political climate. But that the Christians existed cannot be denied. Further, in *Jewish Antiquities* (20.197–203), Josephus writes that the Sanhedrin convened and "brought before them a man named James, the brother of Jesus who was called the Christ."[8]

The fact that Jesus existed, died while Emperor Tiberius was on the throne, and had a mass following in the decades following his death and resurrection cannot be denied. Historical sources show without a shadow of a doubt that Jesus of Nazareth existed in the time and location as described in the New Testament. The sources do not always favorably depict Christians, but this just shows Christianity's influence and threat to the existing Roman structures. Tacitus wrote that Pilate's execution of Jesus resulted in melee and that the "pernicious superstition *broke out afresh* in Judaea."[9] Whether depicted as superstition or gospel was up for interpretation, but that Christianity exploded on the scene following the teachings of Jesus cannot be historically denied.

Jesus' teachings and their far-reaching effects in the first and second centuries are undeniable. But what is equally verifiable is the enduring nature of his influence. For example, have you ever heard of Simeon bar Kosiba?[10] He was considered to be the Messiah by many leading rabbis of his time and was known as "President of Israel." He led an uprising where more than half a million Jews were killed in AD 135, and Bar Kosiba even issued coins and granted land deeds. Yet this man has largely been consigned to obscurity and only rediscovered after some personal letters were unearthed in 1951 near the Dead Sea. Three centuries after Bar Kosiba's death, no one knew him. Also, Acts 5:34-37 mentions two such revolutionaries by the names of Theudas and Judas the Galilean who "claim[ed] to be somebody" and hundreds joined them, but everyone eventually "scattered."

But three centuries after Jesus' death and resurrection, his name was preeminently displayed on the shields of Emperor Constantine's soldiers and came to define this Roman emperor's reign.[11] Compared to Bar Kosiba and other notorious figures from the first and second centuries, Jesus' teachings continue to advance thousands of years after his incarnation. And the name of Jesus continues to dominate conversations around the globe. This is the Jesus whom the New Covenant proclaims as the Son of God and the Word of God.

ORDER AND FORMATION

The twenty-seven books of the New Testament have been categorized in a variety of ways, some by chronological order, others by literary character, and still others by author.[12] The traditional Protestant ordering is as follows, with author and date of composition.

* Matthew
  + Author: the apostle Matthew[13]
  + Date: toward the latter period of AD 45–60 or slightly thereafter[14]
* Mark
  + Author: John Mark, companion of Paul, Barnabas, and Peter
  + Date: either between AD 45–60 or 64–67 (after Peter's martyrdom)[15]
* Luke
  + Author: Luke the physician and Paul's traveling companion
  + Date: written before c. AD 63 when the book of Acts was written[16]
* John
  + Author: the apostle John
  + Date: written toward the end of the first century AD in Ephesus[17]

* Acts

  ✦ Author: Luke the physician and Paul's traveling companion

  ✦ Date: written c. AD 63, after the Gospel of Luke and before Paul's death c. AD 64; narrative ends abruptly with Paul's imprisonment at Rome[18]

* Romans

  ✦ Author: the apostle Paul

  ✦ Date: c. AD 57 from Corinth (see Romans 15:25 with 1 Corinthians 16:1-7)[19]

* 1 Corinthians

  ✦ Author: the apostle Paul

  ✦ Date: c. AD 53–54 from Ephesus (see 1 Corinthians 16:8)

* 2 Corinthians

  ✦ Author: the apostle Paul, along with Timothy

  ✦ Date: c. AD 54–55 from Macedonia, most likely Philippi (see 2 Corinthians 2:13, 7:5)[20]

* Galatians

  ✦ Author: the apostle Paul, along with "all the brothers and sisters" with him (Galatians 1:2)

  ✦ Date: c. AD 55, but perhaps as early as AD 47–48[21]

* Ephesians

  ✦ Author: the apostle Paul

  ✦ Date: c. AD 61–62 perhaps from Rome[22]

* Philippians

  ✦ Author: the apostle Paul, along with Timothy

  ✦ Date: c. AD 62 from Rome[23]

* Colossians
  + Author: the apostle Paul, along with Timothy
  + Date: c. AD 60–61 perhaps from Rome[24]
* 1 Thessalonians
  + Author: the apostle Paul, along with Silas and Timothy
  + Date: c. AD 50–51 from Corinth[25]
* 2 Thessalonians
  + Author: the apostle Paul, along with Silas and Timothy
  + Date: c. AD 51, shortly after writing 1 Thessalonians[26]
* 1 Timothy
  + Author: the apostle Paul
  + Date: c. AD 62–63 from Macedonia[27]
* 2 Timothy
  + Author: the apostle Paul, although Pauline authorship has been doubted
  + Date: c. AD 64 from Rome[28]
* Titus
  + Author: the apostle Paul, although Pauline authorship has been doubted
  + Date: c. AD 62–63 from Macedonia[29]
* Philemon
  + Author: the apostle Paul, along with Timothy
  + Date: c. AD 60–61[30]
* Hebrews—New Testament Antilegomena
  + Author: anonymous

✦ Date: around AD 50–90, most likely before AD 70 when the Second Temple was destroyed[31]

✸ James—New Testament Antilegomena

✦ Author: James, the half brother of Jesus

✦ Date: around AD mid-40s to 90s[32]

✸ 1 Peter

✦ Author: the apostle Peter, but written by Silas (1 Peter 5:12)

✦ Date: c. AD 64–65 from Rome[33]

✸ 2 Peter—New Testament Antilegomena

✦ Author: the apostle Peter, although some questions remain about authorship

✦ Date: before AD 80[34]

✸ 1 John

✦ Author: the apostle John is traditionally noted as the author; verifiably the author is the one who also wrote 2 and 3 John and self-identifies as "the elder"

✦ Date: late AD 80 or 90[35]

✸ 2 John—New Testament Antilegomena

✦ Author: see 1 John

✦ Date: see 1 John

✸ 3 John—New Testament Antilegomena

✦ Author: see 1 John

✦ Date: around AD 90[36]

✸ Jude—New Testament Antilegomena

✦ Author: Jude, the half brother of Jesus and brother of James

+ Date: unknown, although probably in the later first century after AD 70[37]

✳ Revelation—New Testament Antilegomena

+ Author: the apostle John

+ Date: around AD 95[38]

Twenty of these twenty-seven books are considered Homologoumena, and, therefore, have never been disputed regarding their canonicity. The remaining seven are categorized as the disputed books of the Antilegomena: Hebrews, James, 2 Peter, 2 John, 3 John, Jude, and Revelation.[39] Chapter ten walks through each of these seven disputed books, and chapter eleven discusses the compilation process as a whole.

A LOVE RELATIONSHIP

These twenty-seven books comprise the New Covenant, which is a beautiful invitation from God into the fullness of his eternal love. Each book provides a nuanced dimension into God's thoughts and heart toward humankind and is another stroke in a detailed covenant that bespeaks his commitment to us. As we study these books, my prayer is that we would hear God's voice speak peace and reassurance to the very places where we might feel troubled or hurting. If there's a place in your life right now that makes no sense, I pray that God's Word would bring light and clarity.

All analogies fall short, but I hope this one lands correctly: the first confession is like getting married (entering into a covenant), and the second confession is like the marriage itself (living out that covenant). Brian and I got married in September 2005, and that day is forever marked in our hearts and minds. Our wedding was held outdoors, overlooking the beach, and the weather was perfect.

Everything was magical. We sealed our covenant that day in the presence of family and friends, and our union was bound by law and love. Like the first confession that made me wholly the Lord's, I gave all of myself to Brian that September day.

But the beautiful and hard work of marriage started soon after our honeymoon phase ended, and it continues. Making and living out the second confession, like the post-honeymoon phase of our salvation moment, can be both rewarding and arduous. The covenants, both the Old and New, are fulfilled by none other than Jesus. He has done and continues to do it all. But we must wholeheartedly believe in the work of Christ, and that belief extends to accepting the Scriptures as holy writ. Each Bible study, each Sunday sermon, and each exposure of the Scriptures bring us closer to making that second confession. And even after that wholehearted acceptance of God's Word is made, the continual dialogue with the Lord through his Spirit and Word serves as the firm foundation of our lives.

Let us go back to the Scriptures often, not only so that we believe them to be true, but so we can live them out in technicolor in a world that often seems so dark and desperate.

QUESTIONS TO PONDER

1. How does knowing that Jesus was an actual historical figure affect your faith?

2. Which New Testament book or books have been a special part of your faith journey?

10

Ins and Outs of
the New Testament

MY FAMILY AND I were in Israel recently, and I'm still processing our visit. More than a trip or vacation, it was truly a pilgrimage. The sites, the sounds, and the smells still linger. And the people and culture have indelibly marked my mind. In particular, I cannot stop thinking about the Jewish Sabbath. Hearing and reading about this observance were *nothing* like watching it unfold. We traveled from Tiberius to Jerusalem on the Sabbath, and our tour guide went to great lengths to make sure that we were fed and arrived at the hotel at a certain time because so many parts of Israel shut down their businesses on the Sabbath.

The elevators in particular caught my attention. We found out that pressing the elevator buttons is deemed work, which is prohibited on the Sabbath. Many of the elevators are automated—they automatically open and close on every floor during the Sabbath. This means that if you're on the tenth floor, as we were, you have to go through all the floors each way. I thought: *Wow, this is a lot of work* not *to work!* One time when I pressed a button out of habit, several people in the elevator gave me a look of both pity and disapproval. I felt elevator-shamed at that moment—a new feeling for sure.

But the feelings ran deeper. What really remained with me was both respect (for so many people who are extremely earnest to keep God's laws) and concern (to see so many people seeking God in the actual place where Jesus lived but failing to see his deity). Then, I wondered: Where have I missed the truthful teaching of the Scriptures and missed out on an opportunity to enjoy my relationship with God? Maybe I got the Sabbath right, or at least the part about Jesus being the Lord of the Sabbath. But I'm still working out the nuances of a weekly sabbath that truly delights in and honors him. And there are still so (so) many areas in my spiritual walk where I need more biblical truths to undo my wrong thinking.

One way of falsely understanding the Scriptures is simply failing to think about what we think about. Rituals, discipline, and tradition can have a useful and powerful place in our relationship with God. But when these good things become the ultimate goal, they rival God's throne in our hearts. I went through a phase like that when I had very consistent quiet times, and my consistency became far more important than God in my heart. My time with God was more like a performance and something to check off my to-do list. There was very little difference between hitting the gym and hitting the Word.

Then my soul started to feel dry, and I wondered why I felt spiritually emaciated when I was doing the right things. Thankfully God soon brought me back to truly enjoying and savoring time with him, but that experience was a little disorienting. Years later, in a seminary class, I learned language to express that experience. I was both convicted and inspired as our professor insightfully explained that sometimes we send an avatar of sorts to meet with God.[1] It's not our true and authentic self. The social media, well-crafted image of ourselves can sometimes extend to the persona we want God to appreciate. But God knows us better than we know ourselves, so this ruse is ridiculous if we stop and really *think* about it—but sometimes we fail to do just that.

Loving God with all we've got, including the ability to investigate claims and rationally discern truth, is a vital part of the second confession. Once we believe the Scriptures are God-breathed, we get to enter into a lifetime of interacting with the Scriptures. Some of the books of the Bible, however, might have stirred confusion or questions. The same was true of the early church—they had *many* questions, and we are beneficiaries of these questions. There were books in the New Testament era that were questioned, and communities gathered to discuss whether to ultimately include them in the canon. I hope we, too, would read the Bible and investigate its claims, both personally and in community, allowing the investigation to bolster our faith in the Scriptures and our questions to be a blessing to many.

APOSTOLICITY

Celebrities of all walks and eras have claimed their fifteen minutes of fame, but there is no one like Jesus who has dominated our discourse for the past couple millennia. Truly, if all of Jesus' deeds were recorded, the world itself could not contain all the books therein (John 21:25). The sheer amount of dialogue that Jesus has generated is staggering, and some of these writings claim to be Scripture. Out of the countless works, how can we certifiably know what is and is not the Word of God?

For the New Testament, the most crucial criterion is apostolicity.[2] All the books considered canonical had to have been written by an apostle or an apostolic associate, and the date of composition must have been during the apostolic period, which is known as the criteria of antiquity.[3] Other criteria were also considered, such as orthodoxy and catholicity, but apostolicity was the first measure.[4] This meant that well-regarded and useful writings from the first century, such as the *Didache* (or "Teaching") and *1 Clement* (Clement of Rome's letter to Corinthian Christians), commanded "great respect" but failed to get canonized because they were not written by apostles.[5]

Besides the twelve apostles, apostolic authority rested on several others. At the top of the list is Paul of Tarsus, whose Damascus Road experience and subsequent God-given ministries (including penning at least thirteen epistles) rightfully afforded him the title of apostle. There were also James and Jude, both half brothers of Jesus, and all the other authors of the New Testament who claimed apostolic authority outright or through firsthand partnership. For example, Mark was closely associated with Peter (1 Peter 5:13), and the Gospel of Mark has been considered "Peter's Gospel." Further, Mark had his own divinely appointed ministry, such as accompanying Barnabas and Saul as "the word of God continued to spread and flourish" (Acts 12:24-25; 2 Timothy 4:11). The same is said of Luke (author of Luke and Acts), whom Paul called "the beloved physician" and "my fellow worker" (Colossians 4:14; Philemon 24).[6]

The apostles and their close associates took extreme care to record the deeds and words of Jesus. Jesus himself never penned a book, although we can argue that he did author the entire Bible and is the Word himself! But speaking strictly in corporeal terms, Jesus, the Son of Man, never penned words on parchment. Instead, he orally upheld the Old Testament as the Scriptures and taught that he was the fulfillment of the promises therein.

When Jesus referenced the Scriptures, he meant solely the Old Testament since the New Testament had yet to be written. But his teachings also showed that the story was incomplete. The Old Testament left a big cliffhanger for all followers of the God of Abraham, Isaac, and Jacob. The first-century Jews were eagerly awaiting a Savior, and their longing can be felt in the words of John the Baptist, spoken through his disciples, who asked, "Are you the one who is to come, or should we expect someone else?" (Matthew 11:3; Luke 7:19). N. T. Wright well noted, "The great story of the Hebrew scriptures was therefore inevitably read in the Second Temple period as a story in search of a conclusion."[7]

NEW TESTAMENT ANTILEGOMENA

Jesus, the fulfillment of the Scriptures, made it clear that his own words and teachings were on par with the Old Testament. He then promised that the Holy Spirit would empower the apostles to remember all of his teachings and reveal further truth after his ascension. What started as oral tradition became canonized in writing, and the New Testament is the summation and expression of those promises.[8]

From the start, twenty of the twenty-seven New Testament books have never been disputed as canonical. The seven New Testament Antilegomena books were disputed and given semi-canonical status from time to time, but they were rarely deemed anticanonical or uncanonical; these books are Hebrews, James, 2 Peter, 2 John, 3 John, Jude, and Revelation.[9] More than mere terms, these labels allow these books to be seen as heavily discussed rather than ever outright rejected. After careful consideration, each of these seven books were deemed canonical for the reasons that follow.

Hebrews generated controversy because of anonymous author-ship.[10] Some believed that Paul authored this book and hence were eager to canonize it. The only problem with this assertion is that there is no proof that Paul authored Hebrews, and to make that claim is sloppy historical investigation. Also, such a claim need not be made to confirm Hebrews's place in the New Testament canon. The criterion for apostolicity does not mean that the author needed to be an apostle himself, but that there was a close association with an apostle. In Hebrews 2:3, the author states that the gospel was "first announced by the Lord, was confirmed to us by those who heard him." The author of Hebrews, then, was an associate of one who had heard directly from the Lord, so the test of apostolicity applies. This epistle was finally deemed canonical in the fourth century, and Jerome and Augustine were key instruments for this confirmation.[11]

The epistle of *James* was authored by James, the half brother of Jesus, sometime during AD mid-40s to 90s.[12] This book became a source of contention because it supposedly contradicts Paul's teachings on justification by faith. Martin Luther was famously concerned with this book, but he also noted that it is possible to "interpret it according to the sense of the rest of Scriptures."[13] Luther's contemporary and fellow Reformer John Calvin also stated, "It is therefore faith alone which justifies, and yet the faith which justifies is not alone."[14] This message is the heartbeat behind this epistle. Though this epistle garnered serious debates during the Reformation era, its place in the canon was confirmed centuries earlier when Origen, Augustine, Jerome, and Eusebius clarified its "complementary nature" to Paul's epistles.

The epistle of *2 Peter* was questioned by various church leaders, including Calvin, because it was written in a different style from

1 Peter. This concern is assuaged by the fact that writers can employ varying styles, depending on circumstances. Also, while there are differences between Peter's first and second letters, there are also important similarities in language and doctrine. Jerome believed that stylistic differences could have been attributed to varying *amanuensis*, which means that Peter could have used different secretaries to pen his first and second letters.[15] A less important but secondary concern stemmed from the argument that 2 Peter was written in the second century AD, rather than in the first century. But primary sources, such as Qumran literature that dates 2 Peter before AD 80, aptly overturn this objection.[16] Also, many church fathers, including Origen, Eusebius, Jerome, and Augustine, supported the inclusion of this letter into the New Testament canon.[17]

The canonicity of *2 John* and *3 John* was questioned because of their private nature, rather than being general, circular letters to the churches. The book of 2 John is addressed to "the elect lady and her children" and 3 John is written to "the beloved Gaius." Even though these two letters had limited circulation at first, they were never deemed noncanonical. Many of the church fathers in the second century considered these epistles canonical, and they were included in the Muratorian Canon, a second-century Latin list of New Testament writings deemed canonical by Christians. Another objection, however, stemmed from the author identifying himself as an elder rather than an apostle. But 1 Peter 5:1 is another example where the term *elder* is used by an apostle to reference other apostles. Overall, due to these findings and similarity in style between these letters and 1 John, a Johannine authorship was confirmed.[18]

Jude came into question due to verses 9 and 14-15. Verse nine mentions the body of Moses, which some church fathers thought was a reference to the pseudepigraphal *Assumption of Moses*. The same is true for verses 14-15, which mention Enoch and the pseudepigraphal *Book of Enoch*. Mentioning noncanonical books, however, does not equate to the author elevating the cited text as canonical. For example, Paul mentioned pagan poets (Acts 17:28; 1 Corinthians 15:33; Titus 1:12) and clearly did not mean for those texts to be considered canonical.[19] Because these concerns were minimal, the place of this epistle in the canon was never seriously in contention. Jude was widely accepted as canonical in the second century and its influence was also seen in the *Didache*.[20]

Revelation's focus on millennialism (also known as the doctrine of chiliasm) concerned some church leaders in the middle of the third century. Interestingly, Revelation was immediately accepted by the early church in the first century. The "seven churches" undoubtedly wanted to study and preserve the words written to them. But about two hundred years later, Dionysius, the bishop of Alexandria, raised questions about the Apocalypse, and his influence remained until AD 397 when the Council of Carthage was held. Revelation was thereafter deemed canonical, as inspiration (which differs from interpretation) was not in question. This book, along with all the others labeled Antilegomena, raised no further concerns or objections about canonicity once their authorship and authenticity were confirmed.[21]

NEW TESTAMENT APOCRYPHA AND PSEUDEPIGRAPHA

The exact number of books considered New Testament Apocrypha and Pseudepigrapha is hard to pinpoint. The prominent books labeled in both categories are sampled below, although others could easily be included in these lists. The list of pseudepigraphal books is a lot longer than the apocryphal one, even with all the variants, though there is a hazy line between apocryphal and pseudepigraphal. By the ninth century there were purportedly 280 pseudepigraphal books, and even in the first century the list was rather sizable.[22]

Some books, such as the *Gospel According to the Hebrews* (c. AD 65–100), have been thought of as apocryphal, but the correct label would be pseudepigraphal.[23] Pseudepigraphal books were mostly deemed historically valuable but included too much religious lore, exaggerations, or outright heresy to be considered canonical. Some church fathers referenced various pseudepigraphal works in their writings, but they were never accepted as canonical by the orthodox church. Because the dividing lines between useful and heretical were not always clear, the two lists sometimes were intermixed or partially listed in various works.

Various church fathers gave the apocryphal books varying levels of credibility, even though most were not considered canonical. Some, however, appeared in local ecclesiastical canons where they were used scripturally in a particular church for a finite period.

To show the cursory examination that each book can garner, let's consider the *Epistle of Barnabas*. This book was most likely written c. AD 70–79, widely circulated in the second century, and deemed canonical by Clement of Alexandria and Origen.[24] The stylistic writing mirrors Hebrews, although it is more allegorical and mystical. The first few verses read, "Greetings, sons and daughters, in the Name of the Lord who loved us, in peace. Exceedingly and abundantly I rejoice over your blessed and glorious spirit for the greatness and richness of God's ordinances toward you—so innate a grace of the gift of the Spirit you have received." The major problem with this book, however, rested with the important criterion of apostolicity. Also known as the *Epistle of Pseudo-Barnabas*, there was no definitive proof that Barnabas from the book of Acts actually penned the work. Some have attributed it to an unidentified author or a "Barnabas of Alexandria."[25] Deemed more of a treatise than a letter, along with undetermined authorship, this book was later excluded from the canon.[26]

Instead of going through each of the books as such, I've listed some prominent ones here with the purported dates of writing and important aspects in the canonicity debate.[27]

SIGNIFICANT NEW TESTAMENT PSEUDEPIGRAPHAL BOOKS

1. *Gospel of Thomas* (early second century): at least two versions of this book were in circulation; includes fanciful stories such as when Jesus was five years old and played with water by commanding it to gather in one place

2. *Gospel of the Ebionites* (second century): denied the deity of Christ

3. *Gospel of Peter* (second century): considered to be docetic, which means that it denied the humanity of Christ

4. *Protovangelium of James* (late second century): excessive devotion to Mary; fanciful stories about Mary (for example when "Mary was sixteen years old" and "all these mysterious things" happened to her)

5. *Gospel of the Hebrews* (second century): includes a "special" appearance of Jesus to James, and states, erroneously, that

James attended the Last Supper; references the Holy Spirit as our "mother"

6. *Gospel of the Egyptians* (second century): includes outlandish dialogue between Jesus and Salome, the mother of James and John (e.g., "the Lord said to Salome when she inquired: How long shall death prevail? 'As long as ye women bear children . . . '")

7. *Gospel of the Nazarenes* (early second century): contradicts Gospel assertion (e.g., Matthew 12:40) that Jesus spent three days and three nights in the grave; states that the veil of the temple was not torn in two, but that "the lintel of the temple of wondrous size collapsed"[28]

8. *Gospel of Philip* (second century): includes noncanonical sayings of Christ, such as "A disciple one day asked the Lord about something worldly. He replied: Ask thy mother, and she will give thee strange things"[29]

9. *Gospel of Judas* (late second century): includes a "Passion story" about the "mystery" of Judas's betrayal and explains how his "treachery made possible the salvation of all mankind"[30]

10. *Epistle of an Apostle* (second century): odd and heretical sayings such as "He entered into the womb of Mary in the disguise of the angel Gabriel. After his resurrection also He sent His power in the form of Gabriel to free Peter from the prison for one night" and "Christ has also proclaimed the message of salvation in the underworld"[31]

SIGNIFICANT NEW TESTAMENT
APOCRYPHAL BOOKS

1. *Epistle of Barnabas* (c. 70–79): failed to meet the test of apostolicity

2. *Epistle to the Corinthians* (sometimes called *3 Corinthians*, c. AD 96): style of writing markedly different from 1 Corinthians and 2 Corinthians; written anonymously to mainly refute Gnostic influence

3. *Ancient Homily* (c. AD 120–140, also known as *The Second Epistle of Clement*): never circulated widely or deemed canonical

4. *The Shepherd of Hermas* (c. AD 115–140): overly dramatizes spiritual truths; used to aid devotions in the early church but never considered canonical

5. *Didache* (AD 100–120 ; also called *Teaching of the Twelve*): held in high regard by the early church and serves as a good bridge between the Old and New Testaments; deemed more instructional than inspired

6. *Apocalypse of Peter* (c. AD 150; also known as *Revelation of Peter*): vivid descriptions of hell ("flaming mire" and a "lake of pitch and blood and boiling mire"), popular due to these imageries (e.g., influenced Dante's *Inferno*) but never deemed canonical, and some churches did not allow this work to be read

7. *Acts of Paul and Thecla* (AD 170): testimony of an Iconian lady by the name of Thecla, includes obvious elements of fiction and exaggeration

8. *Epistle to the Laodiceans* (perhaps written in the fourth century): mostly deemed a forgery taken from Paul's reference in Colossians 4:15-16

9. *Epistle of Polycarp to the Philippians* (c. AD 108): no new teaching or originality in this work; seems to copy much from Paul's epistle to the Philippians

10. *Seven Epistles of Ignatius* (c. AD 110): peculiar writing style; overly focused on a bishop-centered form of church government[32]

Aside from the books listed here, over ten apocryphal and fifty pseudepigraphal gospels alone have been noted.[33] Many of them include heretical sayings, especially those that misconstrue the Trinity or discount either the deity or humanity of Christ. A good example of such heresy comes from the *Apocryphon of John* (second century) where Jesus, the "Revealer," purportedly states, "I am [the Father]; I am the Mother, I [am the Son]. I am the eternally Existing, the unmixable, [since there is none who] mingles himself with him."[34] Also, some of these writings were actually helpful for religious life and did not contain heresy but simply did not pass the test of canonicity.

KNOWING THE SCRIPTURES

Perhaps reading some of these apocryphal and pseudepigraphal works is unsettling. Or it's reassuring because it attests to the thorough investigative work by the early church fathers. Either way, the sheer volume of these extrabiblical works makes me realize that our society is not the only one inundated with information overload. Sometimes I feel like our twenty-first century world is way too noisy, but these New Testament apocryphal and pseudepigraphal works make me wonder if ancient Christians felt the same way. Certainly, some apocryphal works were and still are valuable (such as the *Didache*), but many of the spurious and counterfeit works made it harder to discern truth from fiction.

In this way, we also might have other things in common with these early Christians. Clearly, many of them were in search of a vital religious life. These fake (nonbiblical) works differ one from another as to why they were written—perhaps some wanted to bring edification to the church, while others wanted to share new or nonconventional ideas. Regardless, the huge attention given to religious life shows that they were awaiting further elucidation and *light*.

This made me think of a recent conversation I had about spiritual enlightenment in the most unexpected place. I was watching Josephine play volleyball, and the tournaments can be long. In the middle of the second and third sets, I chatted with a fellow mom who told me about her "god," who is also her spiritual guide. She showed me his picture (which is on her screensaver) and then told me about his incredible energy, wisdom, and insights.

This mom is looking, like me, for spiritual light in this dark world. And I know we share many other similarities. We both care deeply about our daughters, how they will perform both on and off the courts. We both want the best for our families. We both yearn to live meaningful lives and hope that our spiritual beliefs will propel these efforts. The big difference, of course, is that Jesus, our eternal Guide, is the true light of the world.

I'm still praying for the right time to share about Jesus with this fellow mom. When I mentioned him briefly to her, she said, "Oh yeah, I'm not into religion. I'm more spiritual." I wanted to say, "Jesus hates religiosity too!" And I will, at the right time. But I wonder if, for now, my job is to be God's light by cheering on her daughter, sharing my seat cushion on those hard benches, and listening. And praying for Jesus' light to dawn at just the right time.

QUESTIONS TO PONDER

1. What is a religious tradition you find helpful? And one that might be harmful?

2. Where do you think people most often turn to for spiritual enlightenment apart from the Bible? Why?

11

Compiling
the New Testament

I LOVE THE CHURCH, and I also love our local church. No church is perfect, but Mariners Church comes pretty close. Our church is writing positional papers on important cultural issues, and providing this clarity is one of many reasons why I respect my church so much. In a culture confused by so many issues, the church needs to step up. And ours is doing exactly that.

Our church leaders didn't wake up one morning and randomly decide to write positional papers on cultural issues. Theirs is a thoughtful and loving response to the ideas that are knocking at the church's door—ideas that might have a veneer of truth but are unscriptural and damaging. Twenty-first century Christians are grappling with issues such as abortion, gender identity, and same-sex attraction, among many others.

In the same way, the second-century church responded to their pressing issues at hand. They, like us, responded to issues of morality—but they were also grappling with ideas that aimed at discounting or invalidating the Trinity and/or the deity and humanity of Christ. In particular, Gnosticism and Marcionism made the stakes extremely high; these heretical ideas threatened to unravel the early church. Central tenets of Christianity were up for grabs, and God used these cultural storms, as he always does, to bring greater truth and freedom. Theologian Roger Olson states that "studying false doctrines is a way of protecting the church . . . [since] studying heresies can help us understand and appreciate sound doctrine."[1]

Many church fathers condemned these heresies and confirmed orthodox teachings. They went to the Scriptures to confirm what had been historically upheld as correct doctrine. The church fathers were not doing anything new, but they were upholding already existing scriptural teachings. The church fathers were not the originators of the doctrine, but God used them to confirm and validate biblical teachings.

A modern-day example would be what Mariners Church is doing. We don't believe in the sanctity of life or traditional marriage between one biological man and one biological woman *because* of these positional papers—but, rather, we *already* believe in these things and the positional papers only clarify what has always been embraced. In the same vein, the early church countered heretical ideas because they had embraced the teachings of Jesus penned as Scripture from the start.

Tracing the chronological unfolding of the early church allows us to see how God moves throughout history and humankind. The church fathers played a pivotal role in confirming the New Testament canon, thereby condemning heretical doctrine. To understand what was at stake and the confusion that beset the early church, let's look at some of the second-century heresies and schisms and how the church fathers responded. God's sovereignty is undoubtedly seen through the annals of history and especially during this pivotal season of the early church.

GNOSTICISM, MARCIONISM, AND SCHISMS IN THE SECOND CENTURY

The word *Gnostic*, pronounced "nos-tik," stems from the Greek word *gnōsis*, which means "knowledge." And Gnostics were serious about a certain type of knowledge they considered superior to all others. They emphasized and lauded secret teachings or traditions that were imputed rather than learned. But not everyone was capable of receiving such knowledge. Only those considered "the knowing ones" had the ability to receive this type of instruction. Secret teachings and general secrecy shrouded this movement.[2]

Gnosticism is hard to define because of secrecy and because it became an umbrella term for an attitude rather than a firm set of beliefs. Although different Gnostic teachers often had their own system of thought, overarching principles broadly defined their ideals: the "original divine element" produced spiritual entities, but there was a "fault" that occurred in the divine world.[3] This hiccup created the material world (the existence of matter), but the pure spiritual nature was planted in some select souls. There was a "redeemer" who would reveal the way of escape from the material world for these elect ones and teach them how to return home to the spiritual world.[4]

The main point for our study is to remember that the Gnostics distinguished between an inferior god (whom they called "demiurge" and was responsible for creation) and a superior god (revealed in Jesus as the Redeemer). The only problem with their version of Jesus, however, was that Gnostics claimed he was absolutely transcendent and not incarnate in a human body. Their absolute God would never enter into a human body, which they deemed evil matter. Hence, Gnostics claimed that Jesus only *appeared* to be a human person, but that it was merely an illusion and he remained purely spirit.[5]

The early church responded to Gnostics with vehemence. In fact, what we know of Gnostics initially stemmed solely from their opponents. No matter a heretic or saint, it's not a good thing to be exclusively described by your enemies. Even heretics deserve a fair trial. Unfortunately for Gnostics, orthodox church fathers such as Irenaeus, Clement of Alexandria, Tertullian, Hippolytus, and Epiphanius were the main chroniclers of Gnosticism for centuries; and their inclusion of scant quotations from Gnostic writers were used for polemical purposes. This changed, however, in 1945 when a collection of twelve codices were discovered at Nag Hammadi in Egypt. These, along with some additional "sheets" that were discovered, were original fourth-century Gnostic writings, mostly in a Coptic translation. This twentieth-century discovery helped etch further details of this movement that included Jewish and pagan influences.[6] For example, while the church fathers focused on Gnostics' mythical structures, the Nag Hammadi documents focus more on interpreting the "living spirits." Combined, the church fathers' writings and the Nag Hammadi documents help interpret one another and do not conflict with one another. This is just one of many examples where new archaeological or written findings only corroborate, rather than contradict, what we already know about the Christian faith or tradition.

Other heresies in the second century further plagued the early church. One was called Marcionism, named after Marcion of Asia Minor. He was born c. AD 100 in Sinope, a seaport on the Black Sea, and grew up in the apostolic tradition. Somewhere early in his spiritual journey, however, he became obsessed with the apostle Paul—so much so that Marcion believed that *only* Paul preserved Jesus' teachings without error. Marcion then created his own "bible" by cutting out the Old Testament entirely and including an edited version of the New Testament, which included parts of Luke, ten Pauline epistles, and a host of edited or omitted verses.[7] Marcion never titled his work the New Testament or any real official title. Instead, he referred to the two components as *Gospel* and *Apostle*.[8] He perhaps chose Luke's Gospel because Luke was a close associate of Paul's, although Marcion omitted Luke's name and simply presented it as the Gospel of Christ.

Marcion tried to persuade the church leaders in Rome to embrace his understanding of the gospel. And in case they needed extra encouragement, Marcion made a "handsome donation" to the church. Apparently, Marcion was a successful shipowner on top of his religious pursuits and had ample money to spare. He made this bid in the early years of Emperor Antoninus Pius, who started his rule in AD 138. The more the church leaders in Rome heard Marcion's teachings, however, they became increasingly disturbed. They eventually returned his money, which speaks volumes about how the orthodox church viewed Marcionism.[9]

Other heretical or schismatic ideas, such as Montanism and Encratism, entered the dialogue. Schismatics were those who mostly accepted biblical teachings, but unnecessarily and unhealthily focused on certain rituals. These differing emphases or beliefs caused a schism, or division, within the early church.[10] What should be noted is that various church fathers and bishops established an orthodoxy by AD 200 to properly discredit heretics and schismatics. The term *orthodox* has come to mean many things, including "mainstream" or "traditional." If orthodoxy is thought of as a formalized process—when a group of people form a council and issue a creed—it can appear that orthodoxy was a rather belated reaction against heresy. But if orthodoxy is existing principles that the early church leaders reasserted and restated to counter the rise of heresy, then orthodox beliefs stem from none other than the Scriptures. How the bishops and church fathers steered the church *back* to orthodoxy—the original teachings of Scripture—is a vital part of the compilation of the New Testament.

The orthodox leaders were rightfully alarmed over heresies and schismatics. They worked tirelessly to remove false notions and steer the church back to gospel truth. Their endeavors, along with the political and cultural currents of their day, display how God works sovereignly through his people and through the ages. I hope you'll be amazed, as I was when I saw the sequence of events that allowed for the New Testament canon to come together.

UNFOLDING OF HISTORY

I'll start with the bad news. Biblical historical evidence is scarce between AD 70 to about AD 120. This means that the actions of the church during this time are not readily known through written work.[11] But what is known is certain. This was a key time when Christianity held onto Jewish traditions but also broke free into new theology. In particular, Christians held fast to their Jewish roots in viewing the Scriptures as sacred. As Jesus' ministry was based on the Scriptures (meaning the Old Testament), the Christians, too, were people who were wholly committed to basing their lives on divine revelation written down by men. But the Christians declared something new—they boldly proclaimed that the Jewish Scriptures were incomplete. The apostles and their associates were inspired to pen the New Covenant, which the early church fathers circulated as divine teachings.

Some key historical events expedited these church developments. First of all, the burning of Rome in AD 64 caused untold
torment and brutalities to be unleashed on the Christians—and
this pivotal moment caused Christians to be seen as distinct from
the Jews. Until this point, Christians and Jews were intermingled
in Roman minds as one group[12] and Christians benefited from
something known as *religio licita*. Nations under Roman rule were
required to recognize and worship Roman gods, unless a legal
exception was granted. Because the Jews had unremitting conflicts with the Roman government since the first century BC, the
Romans eventually recognized Judaism as a legal religion. By association, the Christians also received legal protection while under
this Jewish banner.[13]

This legal covering was largely removed, however, in AD 64.
Many people believed that Emperor Nero burned Rome that year
so he could bypass the senate and rebuild the city as he wished.
Tacitus, the Roman historian, wrote that Nero played the fiddle
while watching Rome burn. That's an unsettling scene to imagine
for sure. What's more disconcerting is that Nero blamed the fire
on Christians—making a distinction between them and their
Jewish forebears. When accused of the fire, Nero blamed and
punished the Christians for the inferno. The apostles Paul and
Peter were most likely martyred under Nero's command sometime
between AD 64 and 67, while scores of other Christians were
tortured and martyred as well.[14]

Thereafter, "the name," meaning Christians, went hand-in-hand
in many Roman minds as those stirring up "hatred of the human
race," as Tacitus notes.[15] Even after Nero's death in AD 68, suc-
ceeding Roman emperors, for example Domitian (81–96), Trajan
(98–117), Hadrian (117–138), and Marcus Aurelius (161–180), each

participated in continued persecution of Christians.[16] Persecution continued for over another century, as Christians' individualized identity, separate from the Jews, also advanced.

The next big historic event that further severed Christianity as an "appendage of Judaism" occurred in AD 70. The Jewish temple was destroyed this year when four Roman legions advanced on Jerusalem, led by General Vespasian and later his son Titus. The official siege began in April in the year AD 70, and many Jews could not hold out longer than September. The most zealous Jewish resistance forces relocated to Masada for about three years. But Titus eventually toppled those who had hoped that the mountainous fortress would provide escape from Roman rule. Historian Mark Noll notes that Christianity's independence from Judaism was "greatly accelerated" by the destruction of the Jewish temple and especially the "cessation of the sacrifices" that had defined Jewish worship.[17]

In this subapostolic period—the period after the apostles— great uncertainties loomed large for Christians. But more than any political or military upheaval, what most threatened the early church were heretical and schismatic ideas. Toward the end of the second century AD, Irenaeus, a Christian apologist, listed 217 such religions that had "borrowed liberally from Christian doctrines or practices."[18] By this time, though, Christians were aware of what constituted orthodox teachings. Early on in the subapostolic period, around AD 100, the four Gospels and Paul's writings were circulated among churches as a unit. Other New Testament writings were also circulated but in a more limited fashion at first. Together, these writings were deemed sacred, as noted in Scripture itself.

Second Peter 1:18–2:1 (RSV) is helpful as a theological treatise to see what the early church advocated. This is not a case of using Scripture to validate Scripture but using Scripture as a historical and theological document. Here, Peter notes that the apostles have something more sure than the prophets of the past, for, he says, "we ourselves heard this very voice borne from heaven, for we were with him on the holy mountain." The apostles had "the prophetic word . . . knowing this first of all, that no prophecy of Scripture comes from someone's own interpretation. For no prophecy was ever produced by the will of man, but men spoke from God as they were carried along by the Holy Spirit." Peter goes on to warn that "false prophets also arose among the people, just as there will be false teachers among you, who will secretly bring in destructive heresies, even denying the Master who bought them."

The heresies noted by Peter and those that followed in the subapostolic age played a pivotal role in the formation of the New Testament canon. From the death of the last apostle at the end of the first century, to the end of the second century, heretical and schismatic ideas flourished; it would take more than two hundred years after this to confirm the New Testament canon.[19]

Marcion's list in the second century is the first known published account of the New Testament "canon." As a heretic, his "canonical" list does not accurately reflect the teachings of Christ. Marcion excluded the Old Testament altogether and mostly included Paul's teachings, which he further edited.[20] It would be another two hundred years before the twenty-seven books of the New Testament became formalized by the Councils of Hippo and Carthage in North Africa in the late fourth century.[21] Meanwhile, various lists continued to surface that aimed at delineating canonical boundaries. Some examples are Valentinus's *Gospel of Truth* and the Muratorian Fragment.[22]

Why did it take so long for the *actual* New Testament canon to emerge? The two-hundred-year span should not be unsettling but reassuring for those studying canonicity. The church fathers refused to rush such an important process and worked meticulously and dutifully to discern God's truth. At every turn, as they combed through the myriad of books contending for canonicity, they continued to ask how the central message of that book related to Jesus of Nazareth. Any teachings that deviated from the Gospel narratives of Jesus were immediately jettisoned. Those that were written outside of the apostolic period, even the "good" ones like the *Shepherd of Hermas*, were cut. Any that were not written by an apostle or apostolic associate were not considered. These church fathers are examined in chapter twelve to show how God used these leaders and seismic political and cultural shifts to bring us his New Covenant.

We all feel uneasy when people are used for divine undertakings, because people are imperfect. And the early church leaders were not perfect. Some clashed with one another, others made questionable choices. Tertullian of Carthage, who was a distinguished Christian theologian, famously converted to Montanism in AD 206.[23] Jerome was cranky and ill-tempered.[24] And not all the church fathers agreed with one another on which books should be included in the New Testament canon.

Yet God's sovereignty was never thwarted. God used murderers, adulterers, and cowards throughout Scripture, and he used early church leaders in important ecclesiastical work. The role of the church fathers was indisputably central to the confirmation of the New Testament canon. But a zigzagging progression seems to convey their path more accurately. Sometimes their decisions brought an impasse, other times they resulted in creeds that we still revere today. While they left sizable written records, there are still many unknowns and conjectures.[25]

THE BODY OF CHRIST

Orthodox teachings could sound boring, like old stories from out-of-touch generations. And in our world of instant communication and high speed access, the word *orthodox* can seem stuffy and un-relatable. But Trevin Wax exhorts current-day Christians to embrace orthodox teachings as the church fathers did—and do so with a sense of thrill and adventure. Although we can "become sluggish with the Scriptures; bored with the Bible; drowsy toward doctrine," Wax states that in reality there is nothing "more thrilling" than the "old, old story" of "how a Savior came from glory." He persuasively argues why heresies are actually limiting and not as interesting as fully orthodox doctrine. He provides many steps to making the adventure real, such as embarking on "discovery after discovery, piecing together knowledge as you come to better understand what you believe and why."[26]

In order to flourish as believers in Christ, we need to be taught the truth – which always points back to the orthodox teachings of Jesus. And orthodox teachings can never fully be understood in isolation. There is certainly a place and need for personal worship, but there is equally a need for community. Just as the church fathers needed one another to sift through heretical ideas and hold fast to orthodox ones, we need a larger Christian community to do the same.

Even as we individually stay in the Scriptures, our spiritual community is also a vital part of this exploration. The Scriptures abound with stories of God's children walking together, whether through deserts or revival. We need each other because we are indeed the body of Christ with many parts. Maybe a new church, Bible study, or service event is God's invitation to join in deeper community—and maybe the people we'll meet will become some of our closest friends.

Years ago, my brother, Henry, said yes to an invitation to serve on his church's security team although he had never done this type of work before. Soon he found that he loved driving the golf cart around church keeping everyone safe. He also met a fellow security volunteer who became one of his closest friends. This dear friend was forty years older than Henry and comes from a very different background, yet they became like two peas in a pod. When Henry moved five hundred miles away because of a new job, he searched for a new community. After visiting several churches over several months, he found one that feels right— biblical teaching, worshipful praise, and a multicultural and multi- generational congregation. And I won't be surprised if he's soon driving a golf cart around his new church, finding new brothers on the security team.

There's no doubt that finding community can be hard. I think we've all experienced frustration trying to find community and then trying to make it work once we're there. There will invariably be hurts and misunderstandings. There might be wounds and scars. I know I still bear a few and have inflicted some as well. But I pray for Henry, and I pray for all of us, that God would plant us in our rightful communities. The treasure of community is worth seeking. The perfect and everlasting community we seek awaits us in heaven. Until then, may we invest richly in our church communities and stay true to orthodox teachings—and have a thrilling time doing it.

QUESTIONS TO PONDER

1. What are some key cultural issues (e.g., gender identity, racism, sexism) that you're dealing with today?

2. Do you have a church community? If so, how has your church community strengthened your faith through orthodox teachings? If not, how might God be leading you to a church community this season?

12

The Church Fathers

I KNOW THE WORD *FATHER* can be a loaded term. Some of us had wonderful fathers, and some of us didn't. So when we discuss church fathers, we might bring some baggage to the table. Maybe your father was domineering and authoritarian, or maybe he was too lenient or just outright absent. Although this is not always the case, our levels of trust or suspicion are often affected by those who once held authority over us.

Not just biological fathers, but people with power in the church can also affect the way we see the world, especially the religious or spiritual worlds. All too often we hear about yet another church leader who has fallen into immorality and sometimes criminality. God's Word never sugarcoats this type of abuse. One story I read often to find comfort is found in 1 Samuel, where the prophet Samuel deals with Hophni and Phinehas. These men were priests of the Lord—akin to being church fathers—and they were also sons of Eli, the high priest who judged Israel for forty years. Yet they used their positions to engage in sexual liaisons with women, steal the offerings, and take the fattest portions for themselves (1 Samuel 1:3; 2:22-25, 29). Unfortunately Hophni and Phinehas would not be the last priests (or pastors) to hurt people by misusing God's name.

I want to be like Samuel. He wasn't perfect, but he stayed faithful and kept his eyes on God. Despite the chaos going on around him and the abuses of authority by the sons of the high priests (who outranked Samuel, who was very young at the time), "the boy Samuel continued to grow in stature and in favor with the LORD and with people." The Bible reiterates, "The Lord was with Samuel as he grew up." God kept Samuel faithful and "let none of Samuel's words fall to the ground" (1 Samuel 2:26, 1 Samuel 3:19).

Most of the time, news (whether current or historical) focuses on the negative. As a historian, I'm aware that many historical studies center on conflicts, wars, and struggles. But the heroes cannot be muted. Some might not get their names memorialized or their likeness reflected on a statue, but God knows them each by name—and he raises up women and men in every generation to showcase his righteousness and love. While God alone is the perfect One, he invites people into the unfolding plan of redemption that nothing, not even the gates of Hades, can thwart (Matthew 16:18). And God's sovereignty is seen both in the Bible as well as in those he used to confirm its canonicity.

THE FIRST AND SECOND CENTURIES

After Jesus' resurrection c. AD 30, the next seventy years or so were spent establishing the early church.[1] During this time the apostolic writings were penned. All twenty-seven books of the New Testament were written, copied, and circulated before the close of the first century AD,[2] and the church fathers immediately commented on these writings, using the traditions of the apostles themselves.

Let's pause and look at the Bible as a purely historical document. The Bible states that during the first century, Scripture itself was written, collected, sorted, read, and circulated (2 Peter 3:15-16; 1 Thessalonians 2:13; 5:27; Revelation 1:3; Colossians 4:16; Revelation 1:11). Even if the New Testament isn't accepted as God's Word at this point, what the early church wrote, deemed sacred, and circulated should not be missed.

The New Testament self-identifies as Scripture and quotes different parts of Scripture with the same level of authority. For example, 1 Timothy 5:18 quotes from Luke 10:7 with the same type of authority used to reference the Old Testament—and there are many other such examples. Either the New Testament is a fabrication and falsely testifies of itself, or what it declares is true.

The church fathers believed that the New Testament writings were indeed the Word of God and referenced them as canonical starting in the first century. In fact, every book of the New Testament is referenced by an authoritative first- or second-century work. This reference list brings the point home—each New Testament book is placed alongside first- and second-century writings considered to be the earliest orthodox writings from the church fathers.

Matthew—*Epistle of Pseudo-Barnabas* (c. 70–79); *Didache* (c. 70–130)

Mark—*Epistle of Pseudo-Barnabas*; Papias's *Interpretation of the Oracles of the Lord* (c. 120)

Luke—*Muratorian Fragment* (170–180)

John—Papias's *Interpretation of the Oracles*; *Muratorian Fragment*

Acts—*Muratorian Fragment*; *Shepherd of Hermas*

Romans—Clement of Rome's *Epistle to the Corinthians*; Polycarp's *Epistle to the Philippians*; *Didache*

1 Corinthians—*Didache*; *Shepherd of Hermas*

2 Corinthians—Polycarp's *Philippians*; *Shepherd of Hermas*; *Epistle to Diognetus*

Galatians—Polycarp's *Philippians*; *Epistle to Diognetus*

Ephesians—Clement of Rome's *1 Corinthians*; Ignatius's *Smyrnaeans*; alluded to in *Epistle of Pseudo-Barnabas*

Philippians—Polycarp's *Philippians*; *Shepherd of Hermas*; Ignatius's *Smyrnaeans*

Colossians—Polycarp's *Philippians*; Ignatius's *Ephesians*; *Epistle to Diognetus*

1 Thessalonians—*Shepherd of Hermas*; *Didache*; Ignatius's works on *Ephesians* and *Romans*

2 Thessalonians—Ignatius's *Philadelphians*; Polycarp's *Philippians*; *Dionysius of Corinth*

1 Timothy—Clement's *1 Corinthians*; Polycarp's *Philippians*; *Shepherd of Hermas*; *Didache*

2 Timothy—*Pseudo-Barnabas*; *Shepherd of Hermas*

Titus—Clement's *1 Corinthians*; *Pseudo-Barnabas*; *Epistle to Diognetus*

Philemon—*Muratorian Fragment*

Hebrews—Clement's *1 Corinthians*; *Ancient Homily* (often called Clement's *2 Corinthians*); *Shepherd of Hermas*

James—Clement's *1 Corinthians; Shepherd of Hermas*

1 Peter—*Pseudo-Barnabas; Shepherd of Hermas*

2 Peter—Clement's *1 Corinthians*; *Pseudo-Barnabas*

1 John—*Shepherd of Hermas*

2 John—Polycarp's *Philippians*; *Muratorian Fragment*

3 John—*Muratorian Fragment*

Jude—*Muratorian Fragment*; *The Martyrdom of St. Polycarp*

Revelation—*Didache*; *Shepherd of Hermas*[3]

The point of this list is that every single book of the New Testament was considered sacred from the start. Not one book was omitted when the church fathers wrote about the divine teachings of Jesus. Some extrabiblical works, such as the *Shepherd of Hermas* and the *Didache*, circulated during this time along with the twenty-seven books of the New Testament, but eventually only the twenty-seven books were deemed canonical.

Let me share an analogy. My brother recently applied for a highly-competitive job, and there were several hundred applicants. The office eventually whittled down the list to a handful for in-person interviews, then just three applicants for an all-day interview. At any point, if someone was cut from the list, he or she would no longer be in the running for the position. The same analogy was true of the twenty-seven books of the New Testament. Several extrabiblical writings were initially reviewed and revered, but every book except the twenty-seven was eventually omitted from the canon after careful consideration. At no point were any of these twenty-seven books rejected. Every single one of the books in the New Testament canon had always and continues to remain in the canonical list.

Sure, there were several New Testament books that came up for heated debates (as all rigorous scholarship demands), as discussed in chapter ten, but none were ever outright rejected by the church fathers.

By the dawn of the second century, all the apostles had passed away, and the church fathers picked up the work of the early church in important ways. The most fundamental was using the New Testament books as their mainstay; Communion, worship, tithing, and other such observances were never devoid of the apostles' teachings. Also, church fathers cited the New Testament in their struggles against heretical groups. Whether they were at ideological odds with those outside the church or trying to exhort those within to abstain from vices, the church fathers used scriptural precepts to make their points.[4]

CHURCH FATHERS POLYCARP, JUSTIN MARTYR, AND OTHERS

Without further ado, let's meet some of the church fathers. There's not enough time or space to discuss them all, but we'll focus on several of the major leaders of their time—their primary contributions to the early church and confirmation of the New Testament canon.

Polycarp. The first to make our list is Polycarp, largely because he is a natural bridge between the apostles and church fathers. Polycarp was a student of the apostle John and became the bishop of Smyrna. He eventually penned his own writings, including his own letter to the Philippians.[5] In this letter, Polycarp echoed the words of the apostles John, Paul, and Peter, but for his contemporary context, for encouragement and edification.

To the Philippians is an important part of the "Apostolic Fathers."[6] This term was coined in the late seventeenth century to denote the early church writers but later came to include church documents such as the *Didache*.[7] Hence, *Apostolic Fathers* is also synonymous with the earliest orthodox writings—excluding the New Testament.[8] Here we see that the earliest church writings corroborated the teachings of the New Testament.

As a disciple of the apostle John, Polycarp was venerated and sought after. For example, Ignatius, bishop of Antioch, had been arrested by the emperor Trajan (98–117), and he wrote to the church in Rome pleading with them not to intervene in his upcoming execution. With martyrdom imminent, Ignatius penned seven letters with both urgency and emotion—and one of these letters was addressed to Polycarp.[9] Also, there is a letter from the church of Smyrna sent to the church of Philomelium titled *The Martyrdom of Polycarp*.[10] Polycarp is considered a representative of the early church fathers who faithfully carried on the lives and teaching of the apostles until he was burned to death in c. AD 155.[11] Until the end, Polycarp's own writings testify to these assertions, as seen in his references to the following New Testament passages: Matthew 5:13, Mark 9:35, Acts 2:24, Romans 12:10, 1 Corinthians 6:2, and the list goes on.[12]

Justin Martyr. Also known as Justin the Philosopher, Justin Martyr assumed an important role in the early church. He was born around AD 100, raised by pagan parents, and his initial studies focused on Platonic, Stoic, and other philosophies of his day. But he came to faith around 130 after coming to realize that "this philosophy" about Jesus was alone "true and profitable."[13] He spent the balance of his life writing about and defending the Christian faith. He remained both philosopher and disciple, as he integrated faith and reason into his writings. His surviving works are two *Apologies* and a *Dialogue with Trypho.*[14]

He is known as one of Christianity's first and most important apologists, defending the Christian faith as the "oldest, truest and most divine of all philosophies."[15] In all of his writings, Justin Martyr quoted heavily from the Bible, with over 330 citations from and an additional 260 allusions to the New Testament (examples include Matthew 3:17; Luke 22:19; John 3:3-5).[16] He remained a true witness to Jesus until the end of his life, when he was martyred in Rome around AD 165.

The early church fathers meticulously divided the sacred from the profane, the canonical from noncanonical, because their lives depended on it. They were willing to stake their entire lives on the teachings of the apostles, even to the point of death. The word *martyr* is the Greek word for "witness," and the New Testament uses this term for those who had witnessed the acts of Jesus. For example, in Luke's writings, a witness was someone who had seen and could personally attest to the resurrection of Jesus.[17] True to these terms, many of the early church fathers both were witnesses to and died proclaiming the truth about Jesus.

Although martyrdom had Jewish precedents, the early church experienced it acutely. From the apostles to the early church fathers, martyrdom became embedded in the church's birth. The Bible itself attests to the martyrdom of Stephen in the book of Acts, as well as the apostle Paul who penned many of his letters while awaiting trial and foreseeing his own execution. They all followed the way of Jesus, who was the first and ultimate martyr of Christianity.

Before closing this section, I'll end by listing some other church fathers born in the second century with some of their contributions and controversies. Again, these church fathers reveal both the heights and limits of human agency while showcasing the sovereignty of God.

Tatian (c. 110–172) was an Assyrian Christian and student of Justin Martyr. He condemned pagan philosophies and defended the Christian faith in his *Oratio*. He's mostly known for his *Diatessaron*, which was a harmony of the gospels. Tatian, however, came under Gnostic influence after Justin Martyr's death. Tatian was excommunicated from the church 172.[18]

Irenaeus (c. 130–202) was the first church father to use the entire New Testament in his writings. This means that his work testified that all of the books in the New Testament canon today were corroborated by the second-century church. One of his most famous works, *Against Heresies*, sought to undermine Gnosticism and other heresies. He quoted often from the New Testament and also demonstrated its continuity with the Old Testament.[19]

Clement of Alexandria (c. 150–215) quoted liberally from both the Old and New Testaments in his work.[20] The only books he excluded from the Bible are Philemon, James, and 2 Peter from the New Testament, and Ruth and Song of Solomon from the Old Testament. His writings, however, are sometimes lacking clarity, hard to follow, or erroneous in citations.

Tertullian (c. 160–220) is known as the "Father of Latin Christianity," although his writings were both in Latin and Greek. He sided with the Montanists and condemned worldliness in the church. He published many works and quoted from Scripture often. There are more than 7,200 New Testament references in his writings, although not all of his references are correct. He had a brilliant mind, also practiced law, and coined the term *Trinity* toward the end of the second century.[21]

Origen (c. 185–254) authored more than six thousand writings and books, making him the most prolific author in the early church. His most notable works are the *Hexapla, De Principiis*, and *Against Celsus*. He referenced nearly eighteen thousand New Testament quotations, with 95 percent taken from the Gospels and Pauline epistles.[22]

Cyprian (c. 195/200–258) could have been born at the turn of the third century, but we'll sneak him in at the end of our list of the second century. Cyprian of Carthage authored eighty-one letters and twelve treatises. He referenced the Old Testament about 740 times and New Testament nearly 1,030 times (all except Philemon and 2 John), and his citations are carefully observed and accurate.[23]

Just from these church fathers alone, there were over thirty thousand references to the New Testament!

LET'S STAY FAITHFUL

The church fathers fought the good fight by holding on to truth, by holding on to the Scriptures over heresy. They examined the Old and New Testaments with rigor, and they turned to Scripture for light. Their paths were not lit by feelings, but by faith that comes from the Word of God. And the church fathers remind us that loving God with our minds, not our feelings, is a critical way of adhering to correct doctrine.

For the Hophnis and Phinehases, there are the Samuels, because God knows how to keep his people faithful. The prophet Elijah thought he was the only faithful servant of the Lord, but God told him that he had reserved seven thousand who had never bowed down to pagan gods. And I know there are the proverbial seven thousand faithful ones today. Amy Carmichael, Billy Graham, Mother Teresa, and many others remained faithful to the truth of the Scriptures. Each lived by faith and not by feelings, making sure that they tuned their lives to God's message and not the world's.

Mother Teresa famously went through trials of feeling alienated from God. She had experienced intimacy with God; "'Come be My light,' Jesus had requested of her." She left all to be "that light of God's love" for those "experiencing darkness," but paradoxically "she herself would live in 'terrible darkness.'" Mother Teresa wrote, "Darkness is such that I really do not see. . . . the place of God in my soul is blank. . . . He is not there. . . . God does not want me." She felt utterly forsaken and alienated from God, and she said of this void and separation, "The torture and pain I can't explain." This darkness initially blindsided her and she wondered if she had hidden sin or had gone astray. But she came to ultimately conclude that God's love was greater than the measure of feelings and her suffering was an invitation from God to share "in the Passion of Christ on the Cross." Despite the excruciating pain, Mother Teresa "radiated remarkable joy and love" and "glowed with a kind of 'luminosity'" because her light reflected *the* light (John 1:9).[24]

In a world of darkness, I pray that the Scriptures would be our light. There will invariably be seasons of darkness and confusion, but may we turn to *the* light as did Mother Teresa. By doing so, we emulate the church fathers, who emulated Jesus, by building their lives on correct doctrine based on the Word alone. Sometimes when I'm especially confused, I'll turn on Scripture (instead of blasting '80s music) when I'm driving, putting on makeup, or doing chores. Listening to a podcast or music is good (especially #1 hits of the '80s). But there's nothing like Scripture to lift my spirits and bring illumination, because the Word invites Jesus himself into our midst, and Jesus loves and waits for our invitation.

QUESTIONS TO PONDER

1. Which of the church fathers' writings or thoughts most resonate with you? How did God use the church fathers individually and collectively in the process of canonization?

2. The world is a broken place, with many leaders who have failed to do good. But there are the faithful ones. Who has demonstrated faithful leadership in your life, whether personally or in the church? How might God want to use you to encourage this person?

13

Completing the Canon

ONE OF MY FAVORITE BOOKS is *What If?* In it, key historical moments are coupled with a riveting "What if?"[1] For example, what if there was no fog to cover the Patriot soldiers at the Battle of York in August 1776? Historian David McCullough uses an incredible amount of Revolutionary data to predict that George Washington and his men would have been captured and America would not have been born.[2] Another example—what if the tempestuous storm hadn't receded briefly on June 6, 1945, and the D-day invasion in Normandy had failed? Historian Stephen Ambrose digs into both geopolitical and military evidence to conclude that disaster on epic proportions would have ensued—perhaps with Hitler and Stalin rejoining forces, the Communists controlling the entire European continent, or atomic bombs exploding over German cities later that same summer.[3]

My favorite what-if comes from historian William McNeill, who ponders what would have happened if Sennacherib, king of Assyria, had invaded Judah in 701 BC. Without exaggeration, McNeill believes this is "the greatest might-have-been of all military history."[4] For if Sennacherib would have pressed on, "Judaism would have disappeared from the face of the earth and the two daughter religions of Christianity and Islam could not possibly have come into existence. In short, our world would be profoundly different in ways we cannot really imagine."[5]

Using historical facts, McNeill delivers a persuasive argument as to how easily the Assyrians could have demolished Jerusalem—but they didn't. There was a mysterious illness that plagued the Assyrian troops, which caused the invaders to retreat. Sennacherib, however, wanted to rewrite history and pretend he ransacked Jerusalem. He even commissioned an inscription of his "conquest" on his palace walls in Nineveh. But McNeill asserts that the carvings were "propaganda rather than sober history."[6]

McNeill also sets the historical stage by citing numerous facts, all which substantiate the Bible: Hezekiah ruled 715–687 BC; Isaiah, son of Amoz, was the most important prophet in his day; Manasseh, Hezekiah's son, ruled 686–642 BC; Judah's autonomy collapsed in 586 BC when Nebuchadnezzar, King of Babylon, captured Jerusalem and destroyed the temple built by Solomon; and so on.[7]

McNeill's observations of the historical unfolding are very interesting. First, he notes that Manasseh was "prudent" to "come to terms with alien gods." He also states that "for those of us who are disinclined to believe in miracles, the biblical account of how Hezekiah prepared for the Assyrian attack on Jerusalem contains some tantalizing hints that suggest entirely mundane factors that may have provoked epidemic among the besieging Assyrians." McNeill notes that some archaeologists believe that Hezekiah constructed a six-hundred-foot tunnel that carries water from the spring of Gihon to just outside Jerusalem's ancient walls. And this waterway could have contained contaminated water which caused widespread infection among the Assyrian soldiers. Citing from

2 Chronicles 32:2-4, McNeill states that Hezekiah's decision to "stop the fountains" from the springs that were outside the city could have been a deciding factor in all this.[8]

Although McNeill professes to not believe in miracles, he references 2 Kings 18–19, 2 Chronicles 32, and Isaiah 36–37, and states that the "three accounts agree in all the essentials." McNeill also relays the prayers and faith of Hezekiah, but concludes that the difficulty in finding "enough drinking water in Jerusalem's dry environs may have had more to do with Assyrian retreat than the miracle recorded in the Bible."[9]

Historical interpretation is subjective, but the historical facts that corroborate the Bible are not. This what-if should bolster our faith that the biblical account of the siege is historically and archaeologically reliable and accurate. And as believers and followers of Hezekiah's God, we know that he does indeed work miracles! Personally, as a historian and a believer in miracles, I don't think the two hypotheses are mutually exclusive. Why couldn't both be plausible? God could use contaminated water for his divine purposes.

Using the same historical tools as these preeminent historians, let's pose our own hypothetical: What if the church fathers got it wrong? What if the key Christian councils misheard God? Although these questions veer from historical facts alone and more toward interpretation, these are reasonable questions, especially when so much depends on the answer. Tracing the military, political, and religious events prior to the watershed Council of Nicaea in AD 325 can help establish our historical analysis.

THE NEW TESTAMENT CANON LEADING INTO
THE THIRD AND FOURTH CENTURIES

We saw in chapter eleven that the first known "canon" of Christian writings initially began with Marcion. He omitted the entire Old Testament and cut out large portions of the New Testament, keeping only those he thought related to the apostle Paul. Clearly this list was not an accurate representation of Jesus or of Christianity's Jewish heritage. Nonetheless, the idea of compiling first-century religious writings was first noted here by Marcion around AD 144 near Rome.

Others mimicked the idea of a list soon thereafter, and the next earliest list we have was also from Rome, dating around the end of the second century. This list is known as the Muratorian Fragment because Lodovico Antonia Muratori was the eighteenth-century priest and archaeologist who discovered it. The Muratorian Fragment was first published in 1740 and is very close to our current New Testament.[10] Going into the third century, these lists proliferated, with many overlapping in content. For example, Origen (around AD 185–254) from Alexandria used all twenty-seven New Testament books but noted lingering disputes over Hebrews, James, 2 Peter, 2 John, 3 John, and Revelation. Eusebius, who was a church historian, noted in particular that the book of Revelation caused some people concern because of authorship; initially some were not sure if the apostle John really penned Revelation, but this concern was put to rest.

Despite these conversations, the third century witnessed the church continuing to circulate all twenty-seven books of the New Testament that we have today.[11] This century was also marked by great intellectual activities in general, with the Bible inspiring much dialogue. For example, Origen's masterful

Hexapla compared six versions of the Hebrew Old Testament, side-by-side, one line at a time.[12] But a more careful selection process was needed because this was also when apocryphal and pseudepigraphical works were on the rise. The need to distinguish between works considered authentic and those considered spurious forced the issue of canonicity to the fore throughout the third century.

In the same century, Christians traveled to new lands, spurred in part by persecution and in part by missionary work. Settling into new territories and founding new places of worship further caused Christians to reassess what they considered core doctrine and teachings. The need for distinguishing between the canonical and other religious writings became vital as the Christian message spread to new cultures in the third century.[13]

The fourth century brought great persecution of Christians by Diocletian (302/3) and Maximian (313), which initially seemed like a setback to confirming the New Testament canon. The destruction of biblical manuscripts under Decius's and Diocletian's rules was especially systematic and widespread. Diocletian gave a specific edict in 302 to ferret out and destroy all copies of Scripture as well as other church books, with only the Caesarean library left untouched. Unfortunately, this library, too, was subsequently destroyed.[14]

Throughout the Roman Empire, Christians witnessed their churches and the Scriptures being burned to ashes. Eusebius of Caesarea notes an incident in March 303 when Diocletian ordered "the razing of the churches to the ground and the destruction by fire of the Scriptures."[15] Christians like Lactantius (240–320) lost their teaching positions, and Eusebius notes that those who held high positions would "lose all civil rights" and "be deprived of their liberty." If these threats were not enough, Christians would be "committed to prison, and then afterwards compelled by every kind of device to" capitulate to pagan practices.[16] Light dawned, however, for Christians in the most unexpected place: in the heart of a pagan Roman emperor who would embrace Christ in dramatic fashion.

THE COUNCIL OF NICAEA

Let's set a historical stage: The year was AD 325, nearly three centuries after the death and resurrection of Jesus. Yet the world was still abuzz about him. Was he fully God and fully divine? Was he a mere man? Or did he fall somewhere between the two? In AD 318, Arius (c. 250–336), a presbyter from Alexandria in Egypt, started teaching that Christ was somewhere between these two paradigms. Arius's Jesus was more than human, possessing divine qualities, but he was less than fully divine and subordinate to God the Father. The years between 318 and 325 were filled with debates and letters arguing between Arianism—the teachings of Arius—and orthodox teachings about Jesus.[17]

Arianism infiltrated Christian circles, and his teachings of heresy were far more subtle and subversive than others. If Marcion cut out large portions of Scripture, Arius quoted from the Bible often and revealed his depth of knowledge of both the Old and New Testaments. Although Arius's interpretation of Scripture heavily relied on extrapolations, he still revealed a familiarity and facility with the Bible. Arius's message was also popularized through hymns and chants such as, "The uncreated God has made the Son, A beginning of things created, And by adoption has God made the Son, Into an advancement to himself."[18]

The growth of Arianism intersected with the rise of a new Roman emperor named Constantine (c. 288–337), who played a pivotal role in confirming orthodox Christian beliefs. Constantine had served pagan gods but turned to his mother's God, the God of the Christians, after he had a radical conversion experience spurred by a dream. The dream as well as its timing are noteworthy.

God appeared to Constantine in his sleep on the night before the battle at Milvian Bridge in 312, where Constantine met with one of his major rivals, Maxentius. In this dream, the Christian symbol (✸), taken from the first two Greek letters of Christ's name, was emblazoned in the sky, accompanied by the words "With this you will conquer." He was also instructed to make its likeness as a covering in battle. Complying right away, Constantine put this symbol on all the shields of his soldiers and rode to victory the next day against Maxentius, ascending in power over the Roman Empire. Constantine's conversion and commitment to Christianity were pivotal in the establishment of the church and confirmation of the New Testament canon.[19]

At this point, Constantine shared his power with Licinius, and he immediately sought Licinius's support to legalize the Christian faith and undo the damage wreaked by Diocletian. Constantine eventually ordered fifty copies of the Scriptures to be penned,[20] and he paid attention to the internal friction within the church. As early as 314, Constantine asked several bishops to intervene in some church disputes, and he himself heard and ruled over the appeals in some of these cases. Unity of the church was of utmost importance to Constantine.[21]

It's not a surprise, then, that Constantine made a bold move to bring healing and clarity to the church regarding Arianism. The Arian controversy caused much damage to the church's unity and became a seismic threat to both church doctrine and the Christian community. Hence, Constantine used his powers as emperor and a Christian to put a stop to Arianism by calling a meeting that would decisively denounce the heretics and rightly affirm Christian teachings.

Unlike religious meetings called by bishops or local presbyters, this one had the backing of the Roman Empire: it was called by the emperor himself. This pivotal council took place on May 20, 325, in Nicaea, which was near Constantine's military head-quarters. It was called just a year after Constantine had secured his rule from all other political foes and become the sole emperor of Rome.[22]

At the heart of this meeting was Jesus' identity. Jesus is iden-tified throughout the New Testament as the Son of God, the Word of God, and the Son of Man.[23] Arius adamantly asserted that these descriptions proved that Jesus was "begotten" from the Father, in essence was a created being. But if Arianism proved true, the heart of Christianity no longer held up. Many who took the orthodox position pondered how a created being could pos-sibly provide adequate atonement for humanity's sins. A subor-dinated Christ could never pay the penalty for *all* of humankind—any other sacrifice except God *himself* falls short of a perfect sacrifice.[24]

At the Council of Nicaea, key bishops from various regions came to weigh in on the matter. The bishops from Rome, Car-thage, Gaul, and Persia were among those in attendance. And Athanasius, a young assistant at the time, came to support Bishop Alexander from Alexandria. Not all the bishops were of one mind as to the seriousness of Arianism or the best way to uproot the heresy. But they all agreed on the basics of Christian faith, which they based on a clear and straightforward translation of the Scriptures.

Arianism, on the other hand, relied heavily on conjecture. Arius relied on passages such as John 14:28, where Jesus states that the Father is "greater" than he, or other passages where Jesus' humanity, such as suffering from fatigue or thirst, are noted. Arius also cites Romans 8:29 and Colossians 1:15, where Jesus is called the "firstborn." Mostly, Arius argued that if God was perfect and the originator of all things, then everything, including the Son, must be subordinate to him. He used these "logical intuitions" to support his view of a subordinated Christ.[25]

The bishops at the Council of Nicaea responded that:

1. Christ was *true God from true God.*

2. Christ was *consubstantial with the Father.* [The word used here was the Greek word *homoousios,* implying that Christ was truly "very God of very God," affirming John 10:30 which states "I and the Father are one."]

3. Christ was *begotten, not made.* [He was never a created being and has been the Son of God from eternity.]

4. Christ became human *for us humans and for our salvation.*[26]

At first, some words (such as *homoousios* and *consubstantial*) caused some confusion and pushback. But eventually the Nicene Creed was accepted by the orthodox leaders. At the heart of rejecting Arianism and embracing the deity of Christ was salvation. Athanasius, who eventually became the bishop of Alexandria, spent the rest of his life defending the principles laid out at Nicaea. He contends in *Of the Incarnation* that all of Christianity and the hope of salvation are lost if Christ failed to be God. Athanasius opens his masterpiece with these words: "Come now, blessed one and true lover of Christ, let us, with faith of our religion, relate also the things concerning the Incarnation of the Word and expound his divine manifestation to us."[27]

Eventually, the orthodox position won full acceptance in 381, when the emperor Theodosius called a council at Constantinople. There the assembled bishops reaffirmed the dominant orthodox ideas presented in Nicaea, and the statement that they slightly modified became known as the Nicene Creed.[28] Included in the revision was the trinitarian doctrine that Jesus as well as the Holy Spirit are fully divine persons.[29]

HISTORICAL INTERPRETATION

How do we interpret these facts? Historian Mark Noll notes that Christians are "likely to interpret the evidence . . . in part . . . [as] human responses to the authentic power of God." He concedes that non-Christians may interpret the same sources with "great respect for the integrity of the early Christians" but ultimately conclude that "the construction of the New Testament [was] guided entirely by actions, attitudes, beliefs, practices, and decisions arising from human circumstances."[30]

Either way, as historian McNeill noted of the siege of Jerusalem in 701 BC, the unfolding of events shows that facts are facts. As long as the facts don't conflict, interpretation *can* include the miraculous. Just like God can use contaminated water (or anything else), he can certainly use people to do his will. In fact, that's exactly what he states in the Scriptures: "The king's heart is like channels of water in the hand of the LORD; He turns it wherever He wishes" (Proverbs 21:1 NASB1995).

The serious threat that Arianism posed to the early church should not be underestimated, nor should the timeframe in which the idea infiltrated the church. The seven years prior to the Council of Nicaea were long and tense, so much so that Constantine made it a point to call this meeting the very year after he gained sole rule over the Roman Empire. Even after 325, Arianism continued to influence the church in the fourth century. Yet, this was hundreds of years after the birth and death of Christ—and thousands of years after the Jewish notion of a messiah—had been established. If Arius were contending to start an entirely *new* religion, that would be one thing; but he asserted that the Christ of the Old Testament and the New was not God himself, and this belief undercuts the very essence of the Judeo-Christian faith.

The very heart of Judaism centers on the coming Messiah who would be the Savior of the world. God would not send a prophet— he had already done that multiple times. Moses, Isaiah, and Jonah are just a few of many examples. But *all* the prophecies about the coming Savior signified that God would send his Son. And when Jesus hung on the cross, he was indicted on this very charge—that he proclaimed to be God himself.

Whether these councils interpreted the Bible as true or not is actually not the main point here. What should be highlighted is that those who discredited Arianism and proclaimed that Jesus is indeed God held to the *orthodox* position—that which had always been true of Judaism and later of Christianity. At the core of both religions is the Savior, who is God himself. Whether people choose to follow Christ is one thing, but to assert that Christianity is anything other than Jesus as the incarnate God is to claim an entirely different religion from Christianity. As Christians, we affirm that the council affirmed the correct theological doctrine about the incarnate Christ. But as historians, we also affirm that the council held true to the integrity of the Judeo-Christian faith, which has always asserted that God's Messiah was God himself.

Despite the struggles with heretical ideas, the fourth century closed with a confirmed New Testament canon. The personhoods of Jesus and the Holy Spirit were clearly established, and any doubts about the New Testament Antilegomena were removed. Each of these books was deemed canonical after careful consideration.[31] By the end of the fourth century, the final twenty-seven books had become standardized as canonical.[32]

In fact, confirmation came before that, when Athanasius penned his Easter letter in 367 and the term *canon* was first officially documented. As bishop of Alexandria, Athanasius worried that a few "simple" people would be "beguiled" by taking the "books termed apocryphal, and to mix them up with the divinely inspired Scripture." Because he was so concerned, Athanasius wrote: "It seems good to me also . . . to set before you the books included in the Canon, and handed down, and accredited as Divine. There are, then, of the Old Testament, twenty-two books in number. . . . And again it is not tedious to speak of the [books] of the New Testament."[33]

Athanasius went on to list each one of the twenty-seven books that we have in our New Testament. The content of the twenty-two Old Testament books amounted to the thirty-nine that we have today, with differences in categorization. The fixing of the New Testament canon was extraordinarily crucial in rooting out heresies and clearly delineating orthodox teaching, and it was indispensable to stabilizing the early church. Along with Athanasius's letter, the councils of Hippo Regius (AD 393) and Carthage (AD 397) listed the full twenty-seven books of the New Testament, thereby officially recognizing the New Testament canon.

"GOD, WHAT IF . . . ?"

From Marcion to Arius, the fact that errant beliefs crept into the early church shouldn't surprise us. After all, the serpent was found in the Garden of Eden, and the apostle Peter said plainly, "There were also false prophets among the people, just as there will be false teachers among you" (2 Peter 2:1). Truth has always existed. It's the heretics who launch wayward ideas by asserting the "What if . . . ?" or "Did God really say . . . ?" Satan's tricks are as old as Adam and Eve, but often old tricks unfortunately work well.

What-ifs can take doctrinal or personal tones. Many of us have sometimes wondered if God is present or will provide for us. Is he truly enough? Is he true to the claims of the Bible—or is it hype?

I've struggled with anxiety and sometimes a host of what-ifs that can plague my mind—and they often dovetail with "Did God really say . . . ?" A few months ago, I was really burdened by a slew of what-ifs. On top of that, I was anxious about an upcoming trip. I had a panic attack while flying years ago while I was pregnant, and it had come out of nowhere. Prior to that, I had flown all over the world by myself with never a second thought. Since then, I've gone through many, many steps to get back on a plane. I've flown both domestically and internationally since, but each flight is covered with an enormous amount of thought, planning, and prayers.

I was in the middle of a round of what-ifs about an upcoming flight, when God seemed to interrupt my thoughts. He spoke into my heart, "What if everything goes well?" That thought was so unlike my usual repertoire that I had to stop and ponder the significance, and this became a turning point for me. God never promised that we wouldn't have hardship, but he promised that he would work all things for our good (Romans 8:28). I was reminded of the many passages in Scripture that promise that God is for me, he plans good things for my life, and he will not give me a stone when I ask for bread. If God gave his Son to die for me, he would surely not withhold anything good from me.

Now, whenever a what-if enters my mind, I think *What if everything goes well?* And things usually do. But if they don't (or not according to my definition of *well*), I know that God really did say that he loves me and will care for me no matter what. I know his Word to be true because he went to such lengths to confirm it.

By the way, that flight turned out to be one of the best ever. I sat next to a lovely woman by the name of Colleen, and in about five minutes I knew that she wasn't just a seat partner but a sister in Christ. We chatted like lifelong friends, and those five hours flew by. Her affectionate term for God is *Papa*, and she would share "I was telling Papa this . . ." or "Papa outdid himself when he . . ." Her love for the Lord was so radiant and beautiful—like the sun that shines and makes everything golden.

The flight back wasn't as great, and there was turbulence, no Colleen, and moments of fear that crept in. But God was near, and he kept me together. Sometimes he answers with sunshine and other times with rain, and I need both for my soul.

QUESTIONS TO PONDER

1. What is one what-if that worries you the most? What might God's Word say about that situation?

2. What if Constantine had not converted to Christianity? How might God have worked to preserve the Scriptures?

14

Answering Challenges to Scripture

WHEN JOSEPHINE AND JD were young, Brian and I made a commitment to be the first point of exposure for important life topics. Especially the bad ones. Drugs, pornography, and internet addiction were among those topics. We also added the good ones, like sex and romance, that have been degraded and twisted by society. I could imagine an acquaintance coming up to them and offering them drugs or a quick look at an "interesting" or "funny" meme that could forever alter their course. We knew this type of exposure was highly probable. Without prior conversations, we were setting up Josephine and JD for confusion or worse. But with a proper introduction to these topics at home, followed up with many conversations and prayers, we gave them tools to fight the good fight. Investigation, facts, sober assessment, and prayer were key to understanding why these topics plague our society and continue to seduce us.

In the same way, I think it's vitally important that the church is the first point of contact for the "bad" news regarding the Bible. I put *bad* in quotes because these topics aren't really bad news. Yet there are topics that the church should teach congregations so they have the proper tools for the work ahead. The worst place for

Josephine and JD to first learn about sex would be at a social gathering without parental supervision. In the same way, the worst place for Christians to learn about variant manuscript copies of the Bible would be when trying to evangelize to a friend. These conversations need to take place in-house before anywhere else. The three topics listed here aren't exhaustive and many others could be added, but I hope they provide a framework for why the seemingly "bad" news of the Bible isn't bad news at all.

"THE AUTOGRAPHS NO LONGER EXIST"

The original writings of both the Old and New Testaments are no longer in existence. Known as *autographs*, these originals have long since disappeared from the earth. The Leningrad Codex is the oldest complete copy of the Old Testament and dates to the eleventh century AD.[1] And the oldest complete copy of an Old Testament book is the Book of Isaiah from the Dead Sea Scrolls in Qumran, dated to 350–100 BC.[2] The oldest complete copy of the New Testament is the Codex Sinaiticus, which dates to c. AD 340–350. And the oldest fragment of the Greek New Testament (including John 18:31-33, 37-38) is called the John Rylands Papyrus and dates to the early to mid-second century AD.[3]

Is it possible to know what the originals conveyed when they no longer exist? The answer is a definitive yes. Although no original copies of the Old or New Testament exist, we can be certain that they were passed on with great fidelity throughout the years. For example, there is an unprecedented number of New Testament copies when compared with other documents from antiquity. In addition to the thousands of Greek manuscripts, there are Latin, Syriac, and Coptic translations of the Gospels. And these copies were found in different geographical locations.[4]

Put in other terms, we have about 650 Greek manuscripts of Homer's *Iliad*, which was "the bible" of ancient Greeks. There was also a long gap between the original composition (c. 800 BC) and the extant manuscripts (c. second and third centuries AD), and many are incomplete and very fragmentary. The *Iliad* has the greatest number of manuscripts in all of ancient literature—that is, with one exception, which is the New Testament. Comparatively, the New Testament has over 5,000 Greek manuscripts and thousands of others in various languages. For example, there are between 8,000 and 10,000 Latin manuscripts and another 8,000 in the Armenian, Ethiopic, and Slavic languages.[5] Taken altogether, these many manuscripts faithfully reflect the New Testament that we have in our possession today.

The oldest surviving fragment of the New Testament is from the Gospel of John. From the style of script, this fragment was dated to about AD 100–150, and can be placed during the reigns of either Emperor Trajan (AD 98–117) or Emperor Hadrian (AD 117–138). Many noted paleographers corroborate this assertion, and one stated that "in no other case is the interval of time between the composition of the book and the date of the earliest manuscripts so short as in that of the New Testament."[6]

The consensus among these manuscripts is overwhelming. A vast majority of these manuscripts corroborate one another. The autographs are discernible because the thousands of copies state virtually the same things. Some scribal errors are noted in a number of manuscripts, but not a single church doctrine has been compromised due to these errors.[7]

"THERE ARE ERRORS IN THE COPIES"

This brings me to our second point. Best-selling author Bart Ehrman wrote a book called *Misquoting Jesus* that looks at textual criticism.[8] Sometimes also called "lower criticism," *textual criticism* investigates various copies of a manuscript to reconstruct an original work that no longer exists. For textual criticism of the New Testament, this involves studying different types of manuscripts, comparing discrepancies among them, and investigating the copying methods. Ehrman argues that New Testament textual criticism has not done a faithful job.[9]

Ehrman contends that the English Bible that most of us possess is a tainted copy that does not accurately reflect the autographs. Ehrman argues that many of the scribes were not professionals and "mistakes, pure and simple" entered into the manuscripts. He also asserts that "slips of the pen, accidental omissions, inadvertent additions, misspelled words, blunders of one sort or another" crept in, along with those who purposefully changed words for personal, theological, or political reasons.[10]

The Greek New Testament has about 140,000 words, with between 300,000 and 400,000 textual variants among them, so there are more textual variants than words in the New Testament.[11] Four hundred thousand is a big number, and it can be unsettling without an explanation. But there are very rational explanations why the Old and New Testament manuscripts can be accepted with certainty.

Because of the tens of thousands of copies of the New Testament, even 400,000 variants averages to only about sixteen variants per manuscript. A vast majority of these errors are trivial and easy to spot. The most common textual variants stem from spelling errors. For example, one is known as the "movable *nu*."

This is akin to adding an *n* at the end of *a* if the next word starts with a vowel in the English language. These, along with other spelling errors, occur from time to time in various manuscripts. Another variant stems from including words that do not alter the meaning of the text or translation. For example, adding a definite article to proper names, such as "*the* Barnabas." Some manuscripts vary in having these articles. There are also word order differences, where inversion of words occurs occasionally. But because Greek is a highly inflected language, word order does not affect the meaning of the text as it would in English.[12]

A majority of the variants are these types of simple errors that do not affect the meaning of the original text. What these variants actually show is how a vast majority of the manuscripts are identical with one another. The tens of thousands of copies of the New Testament corroborate with one another on all doctrinal points—and no core theological issues, such as the deity of Christ, his death, or resurrection, are touched by any of these errors.

The two notable exceptions to such simple errors, as Ehrman points out, are from John 7:53–8:12 (about the woman caught in the act of adultery) and Mark 16:9-20 (commissioning of the disciples). Ehrman is right that these passages were most likely not found in the original writings, and modern Bible translators have always been upfront about these variants. Faithful translations of the Bible bracket these verses with an explanation stating that the earliest manuscripts did not contain them. But even without these passages, the main message of the New Testament remains untouched.

New Testament scholar Daniel Wallace states it well: "Although much emotional baggage is attached to these two texts for many Christians, no essential truths are lost if these verses are inauthentic." He goes on to say, "The abundance of variants is the result of the very large number of remaining New Testament manuscripts, which itself gives a stronger, not weaker, foundation for knowing what the original manuscript said."[13] Several other thoughtful and well-researched books properly discredit Ehrman's claims. Two of my favorites are by Timothy Paul Jones and Craig L. Blomberg (see further reading suggestions at the end of the book).

As with New Testament manuscripts, all original Old Testament ones have long vanished. There are currently over 3,000 Hebrew manuscripts of the Old Testament; 8,000 in the Latin Vulgate; over 1,500 of the Septuagint; and over 65 copies of the Syriac Peshitta. The originals were most likely written on papyrus, and the task of copying the sacred texts was given to a special group of priests. This changed in c. 500 BC when a group of teachers and scholars specializing in the law, known as *soperim*, would meticulously copy the Hebrew text. Then, around AD 100 to 300, the *tannaim* (scribes) carried on the tradition. They had stringent rules, such as no word or letter could be written from memory, and any page with more than three mistakes was destroyed. Some minor errors, such as misspelling or fusing words, did creep in. But these variants have no bearing on the Old Testament messages.[14]

One of the most exciting discoveries confirming the authenticity of the Hebrew Bible occurred in 1947, when two Bedouin shepherds stumbled upon a treasure trove while in search of one of their straying sheep. Inside a cave in Qumran near the Dead Sea, they found jars with ancient scrolls containing manuscript fragments of the Hebrew Bible. In fact, the oldest manuscript fragments we have of the entire Bible come from the Dead

Sea Scrolls, with the oldest manuscript dating to about the third century BC and ending in the first century AD. These manuscript fragments include every Old Testament book except Esther. Just like the thousands of copies of the New Testament manuscripts corroborating the Scriptures we hold today, these fragments verified the Hebrew Bible that Christians inherited from their Jewish tradition.[15] In fact, when the entire scroll of Isaiah was discovered at Qumran, scholars found that the Masoretic Text (common version of today's Hebrew Bible) and the Qumran manuscripts, which are separated by about one thousand years, are virtually identical.[16]

"ARCHAEOLOGY HAS DISPROVED THE BIBLE"

A friend of ours is an atheist, and he claims that archaeology validates his choice. In particular, he has stated that the site of Noah's ark has never been discovered and that's enough proof to disprove the entire Bible. He's right that the actual site has never been definitively proven, and the ark hasn't been located. These points, however, do not prove that this event did not occur. In fact, the opposite holds true. Scores of evidence, especially the *Epic of Gilgamesh* from ancient Mesopotamia, verify that a flood of epic proportions occurred. One point of confusion is that the "mountains of Ararat" has been mistakenly identified as the tallest mountain bordering Turkey and Armenia, which is known as Mount Ararat. Genesis 8:4 notes *Hare Ararat*, which is plural and not singular, and means that the Bible never asserts that the ark necessarily landed on today's Mount Ararat. There are many possibilities as to why the ark no longer exists today. And there is a host of other evidence of the flood, such as the discovery in the early twenty-first century of boats in Abydos, which shows how ancient Egyptians had mastered boat making similar to Noah's by 3000 BC.[17]

While others have similarly claimed that archaeology disproves the Bible, there is much evidence to the contrary. In fact, archaeology provides an additional layer of corroboration with Scripture. For example, academics had thought that the Pool of Bethesda mentioned in John 5:1-15 never existed since such a place had not been found. Yet the Pool of Bethesda was recently excavated about forty feet below ground, and there were five porticoes as John described it.[18] Another example comes from Luke 3:1, which reads: "In the fifteenth year of the reign of Tiberius Caesar—when Pontius Pilate was governor of Judea, Herod tetrarch of Galilee, his brother Philip tetrarch of Ituraea and Trachonitis, and Lysanias tetrarch of Abilene." Luke was thought to have erroneously mentioned Lysanias because most historians recognized him as the ruler of Chalcis about fifty years prior to this mention. But archaeologists later found an inscription from AD 14–37, during the rule of Tiberius, which verifies that Lysanias was tetrarch in Abila near Damascus. This is exactly what Luke had written. It turns out that there were two government officials by the name of Lysanias, one mentioned by Luke and another fifty years earlier.

One archaeologist noted that all together Luke mentions thirty-two countries, fifty-four cities, and nine islands, and not a single error has been found in these geographical locations.[19] The same is true of the many places listed in the Old Testament that corroborate archaeological research. This is a stark comparison to the *Book of Mormon*, where no person, city, or nation mentioned has ever been located.[20]

Lee Strobel makes a great point that faithful archaeological data lends historical credibility to the stories in the Bible. Correct history or theology on their own don't mean that the Bible is God's inspired Word. But without them the Bible can easily devolve into fanciful tales not rooted in reality. The truth, though, is that the Bible has always been grounded in history. Actual events unfolded during specific times in real places involving real people. If these do not bear out, then the question of inspiration cannot be faithfully broached. But the historical and archaeological corroborations to the Bible provide a gateway for seekers of truth to stand on firm footing.

PROPHECIES

The most amazing evidence to the inspiration of Scripture is in the prophecies. There are dozens of prophecies foretold about the coming Messiah throughout the Old Testament, and Jesus is the *only* one who matched these predictions. Interestingly, the Christian Victory Publishing Company of Denver, Colorado, offered a $1,000 reward to anyone who could identify someone who fulfilled just half of the prophecies listed in Fred John Meldau's *Messiah in Both Testaments*. Not a single person came forward. Still, no one can ever match these predictions but Jesus of Nazareth.[21]

Out of the many Old Testament predictions about the coming Messiah, the odds of fulfilling just eight of these are highly unlikely. For example, the Old Testament foretells that the Messiah will be born in Bethlehem, be preceded by a messenger, enter Jerusalem on a donkey, be betrayed by a friend, have his hands and feet pierced, be silent before his accusers, and that his betrayer will get thirty pieces of silver, which would be used to purchase a potter's field. The odds of one person fulfilling all eight of these prophecies are 1 in 100,000,000,000,000,000 (that is seventeen zeros after the one!) according to mathematical analysis. The odds of one person fulfilling forty-eight prophecies are 1 in 10^{157}. Even without a mathematics degree, we can agree that this number is so huge that the odds of one person fulfilling these claims could not have been happenstance.[22]

During my years as a professor, I've come across all sorts of cheating methods, and I'm very wary of doctored documents. For example, students have told me they forgot to submit an assignment but had it completed before the due date. When that claim is made, I send the document to our university's IT department to authenticate when the document was first created. In a similar way, these prophecies are authenticated by the date of their composition. The Hebrew Bible, including these prophecies, was written thousands of years before Jesus' incarnation. That Jesus fulfilled these prophecies should make us pause, at the very least, and consider the statistical probability of such an audacious claim.

All of Scripture points to a single person, and his name is Jesus. From Genesis to Revelation, the Scriptures testify to his love, sacrifice, incarnation, and redemption. If we miss Jesus, we'll miss the point of the Bible. He not only fulfilled all the prophecies of the Old Testament, but he lived a sinless life, provided a substitutionary death for our sins, and rose again from the dead.

One of my all-time favorite quotes about the resurrection comes from Charles Colson:

> I know the resurrection is a fact, and Watergate proved it to me. How? Because 12 men testified they had seen Jesus

raised from the dead, then they proclaimed that truth for 40 years, never once denying it. Every one was beaten, tortured, stoned and put in prison. They would not have endured that if it weren't true. Watergate embroiled 12 of the most powerful men in the world-and they couldn't keep a lie for three weeks. You're telling me 12 apostles could keep a lie for 40 years? Absolutely impossible.[23]

No one would be willing to die for a lie. Either the apostles actually *saw* him, or they didn't. And once they saw the resurrected Christ, there was no turning back.

We serve a resurrected God who conquered death forever so that we could live eternally. The older I get, the more this promise is precious to me. My hope, however, is not based on wishful thinking. It's a mixture of faith and facts: historical data, archaeological evidence, and biblical proof intersecting with the divine voice of our Savior. Mostly, it's based on the *reality* of God's love that's more real and durable than anything tangible. Jesus might not always provide the exact answers that I'm seeking, but he always gives of himself. And I realize anew that his loving presence is the answer I've been searching for all along.

QUESTIONS TO PONDER

1. What is the most difficult question you've encountered while trying to share the gospel?

2. What does God's Word say about this topic?

15

Build on Rock

LAST YEAR I was in prayer when God spoke into my heart, "Build on rock." So, I wrote down those words, as I do when he speaks to me.

build on rock

It wasn't an audible voice, but there was no mistake it was his. Then, after my time in prayer, I walked into the kitchen. Brian was standing there, and he had a look like he was bursting with something to share. He told me that he had a dream where he was standing in front of a plot of land. He was going to build a house, and there were different types of material surrounding him. And he was going to start building the foundation with slabs of rock.

I stood there a little in disbelief. I was still clutching the paper where I had scribbled "build on rock." After Brian was done sharing, I slowly pulled out my paper and explained to him that God had spoken to us the same message. We hurriedly went to our Bibles, opened to Matthew 7:24-27 (NASB), and read,

Therefore everyone who hears these words of Mine and acts on them, will be like a wise man who built his house on the rock. And the rain fell, and the floods came, and the winds blew and slammed against that house; and yet it did not fall, for it had been founded on the rock. And everyone who hears these words of Mine, and does not act on them, will be like a foolish man who built his house on the sand. And the rain fell and the floods came, and the winds blew and slammed against that house; and it fell—and its collapse was great.

Jesus spoke these words as he finished the Sermon on the Mount.[1] After teaching on a host of topics—greed, anxiety, the golden rule, being salt and light in this world, and giving to the poor—Jesus summed up this historic sermon with this directive to build on rock. He was saying that it will profit us little if we merely know these truths but fail to put them into practice.

One of my fears in learning more about the Bible is that it will puff me up with pride. I will be able to quote Scripture, even the references, and I'll know more theology, history, and archaeology than the average person. Outwardly it might look like I'm a "good" Christian because I have impeccable church attendance, tithe regularly, teach Bible studies, and go on mission trips. But I fail to humble myself under the mighty hand of God, and I become wise in my own eyes.

Since that day when Brian and I both were told to "build on rock," I've thought often about how this relates to the second confession. After all, the devil also knows and believes in God's Word. He probably even knows it by heart, if he has a heart. Satan used God's Word to try to tempt Jesus in the wilderness. Several times, the devil said "for it is written" and then quoted Scripture. In many ways, the devil is theologically sound: he knows about God's power, God's love, and God's Word. He also believes in the triune God, for we read in James 2:19 (NASB1995), "You believe that God is one. You do well; the demons also believe, and shudder." Yet we know that an eternal hell awaits the devil and anyone like him.

Jesus asked the Pharisees, "Why do you not understand what I am saying? It is because you cannot hear My word. You are of your father the devil, and you want to do the desires of your father" (John 8:43-44 NASB1995). Jesus told this to the leading religious leaders of his day—to the people who knew the Hebrew Bible inside and out. He told them that they were unable to *hear* his word. And, without mincing words, he told them they were spawn from the devil.

I don't want to be like the devil. I don't want to only believe in God's truth but fail to submit myself to its teachings. I don't want to twist the Word of God so that it gives me license to fulfill my own desires rather than pursue the desires of God. I don't want to engage in a whole bunch of "Christian" activities but fail to love others from the heart (1 Peter 1:22). I don't want to be immunized from the truth because I have just a smidge of it to inoculate me.

OPPOSING FORCES

We should be aware of our opposition. The devil is our adversary who prowls around, seeking people to devour (1 Peter 5:8). One of his main tricks is to steal the Word from being planted in our hearts and minds. Jesus stated that the "evil one comes and snatches away" the word that "was sown in" someone's heart before it could bear fruit (Matthew 13:19). It's like an interception or a heist, where the intended recipient is robbed outright.

Make no mistake about it; when the Word of God is preached, spiritual battle always ensues. The devil knows that our lives are at stake. For we will be powerful and loving people as we continue to believe and live out the Scriptures. We will be filled with the Spirit, bearing much fruit. We will live self-controlled lives, not binging on Netflix and drinking and food and entertainment, but exuding joy, peace, and love. The devil's plan is to steal, kill, and destroy (John 10:10) in any way he can and put a stop to all this.

In C. S. Lewis's *Screwtape Letters*, the senior devil, Screwtape, coaches his nephew, Wormwood, on the ways of evil. Each demon is assigned to a person, called a "patient," whom the assigned demon tries to steer into darkness. Screwtape writes, "It is funny how mortals always picture us as putting things into their minds: in reality our best work is done by keeping things out."[2] The Word of God stands atop this list of things to "keep out" of our minds, for this is the singular vehicle through which meaningful lives are lived. When people "hear the word and accept it," they bear fruit—thirty, sixty, and a hundred times as much (Mark 4:20).

C. S. Lewis wisely noted that we fall into two "equal and opposite errors" regarding "the devils." One is ignoring them and disbelieving their existence; the other is an excessive fascination with them. These are good words to heed as we consider the devil's schemes to keep the Word of God from taking center stage in our lives. The opposition is an undoubted reality, but the greater reality is our Jesus who vanquished death and darkness through his death and resurrection. Although victory is his and awaits us eternally, humankind yearns for Jesus' return when he will usher in his eternal kingdom. Until then, God invites us into this epic battle between darkness and light, and he gives us all we need to remain steadfast in our faith. Let us put on the full armor of God, pick up the sword of the Spirit, which is the Word of God, and get ready for battle (Ephesians 6:17).

IT'S IN WRITING

One way of engaging in battle is hiding. I don't mean cowardly hiding but hiding under the shadow of his wings (Psalm 57:1) and hiding his Word in our hearts (Psalm 119:11). We don't have to strain and labor to bear fruit; we simply need to stay in his Word. Lately I've been trying to read God's Word whenever I feel empty. On certain days, that provides many opportunities to open the Bible. Instead of going to a friend or reading another news feed, I want to go to the only One who has true answers and the power to do something about it. And what I love about the Word is that it's *written*.

I'm not sure about you, but I need things in writing. I forget things all the time. The oral culture of Jesus' time was starkly different from ours, and people committed much to memory back then. In fact, some rabbis became famous for being able to recite the entire Old Testament from memory![3] I struggle with memorizing just a few verses and, to be honest, I can't recall even my closest friends' phone numbers. Maybe you can relate.

God knows that we're forgetful. Even if we have photographic memories and can recite long passages, we still tend to forget his goodness. The Israelites forgot that God parted the Red Sea, and they complained soon after this monumental miracle that God would leave them for dead without water in the desert. God commanded *water* to part, and the Israelites needed *water* to drink. You would think that the Israelites would have deduced that God knows, at the very least, how to deal with water. But they forgot and questioned his love and provision for them.

And we do that too. He provided financially in the past, but we wonder if he's going to come through again. Or, he's provided healing in the past, but we wonder if he's still Jehovah Rapha, the God who heals. Somehow it feels different each time, and it feels different when it's *us* and not someone else. That's why God wrote down his Word for us so that we could go back over and over and be reminded of his hesed love for us.

Hesed means grace or "covenant love."[4] But the meaning is actually so much more. Musician Michael Card wrote an entire book on this one inexpressible word. Card beautifully illustrates that the "ever-incomplete working definition" of hesed can be summarized as "When the person from whom I have a right to expect nothing gives me everything." Further, he states that hesed "marks the transition from despair to hope, from emptiness to a new possibility of becoming filled once more." And understanding hesed, which he believes is the "greatest sacramental word in the Hebrew Bible," is "a lifelong journey."[5] For we cannot exhaustively know God's love in this lifetime.

This type of love goes way beyond feelings—it is loyal, steadfast, and unfailing. And God wanted to seal his hesed love for us in writing. That's why he chose the Bible as his main method of communication to us. His Old and New Covenants are his forever promise to love and take care of us until the end. Our birth certificates, educational degrees, and marriage certificates authenticate and legitimize our standing—all in writing. The Bible is no different. God authored the contract, signed it with his blood, and sealed it with his Spirit so that our standing as his children would never be in doubt.

THE SPEECH IS THE WORD

The Bible is not only a covenant between us and our Creator, but it is the *Logos*. John 1:1 states that "In the beginning was the Word, and the Word was with God, and the Word was God." What does the "Word" mean? We can get help from John Calvin here. He noted that the term *speech* was a better translation of Logos than *word* because it more aptly conveys that the Scriptures reveal God's wisdom, will, and mind.[6] Hence, "In the beginning was the Speech, and the Speech was with God, and the Speech was God."

Have you ever heard a really good speech? JD, Josephine, and I love watching TED Talks and listen to them often. But more than this type of speech, the word *logos* here means speech that reflects someone's mind and character, that reflects the core of someone's heart and soul. This type of speech reveals hidden secrets, future intentions, and deep wishes.

In some ways, I think of the Bible as a reverse-prenuptial agreement. Instead of what we *don't* get, the Bible promises all that God *will* give us because he wants to. When a couple signs a prenuptial agreement, one party goes through a list of assets that are untouchable should the union dissolve. They comb through all that is valuable and try to protect their financial interests at all costs. God is exactly the opposite with us. He combs through the depths of his treasuries to tell us all that he wants to bestow on us. He's all in, he doesn't hold an ounce back, and he's given it all. From the dawn of humankind to his second coming, God pursues us with his hesed love—and the Scriptures are the signed, sealed, and delivered expression of this love.

JESUS, OUR GUIDE

By faith, Christians believe that God is omnipotent. His power is unlimited, including his ability to reveal himself to humankind through written words. By knowledge, Christians augment their faith by understanding the creation of Scripture. God chose over forty human agents, mostly kings, prophets, priests, and apostles, to pen his thoughts and heart for us. Some writers, however, remain unknown. Also, about fifteen hundred years span the writing of the Scriptures, starting with the Pentateuchal narratives during the Middle and Late Bronze ages to the end of the first century AD.[7] The Old Testament was written primarily in Hebrew, with portions of Daniel and Ezra in Aramaic.[8] These thirty-nine books recount the stories from creation, the rise and fall of the Israelite nation, to about four hundred years before Jesus' birth. The New Testament was written in Greek and covers the birth of Christ to the glorious eternal future that awaits all Christians. These twenty-seven books usher in the kingdom of God, even while repeatedly quoting from the Old Testament, revealing the continuity of God's story from the beginning to the end of the ages.

The Christian story is indeed a scandalous one. No one would willingly make this up. If someone were to fabricate a religion, they would never choose the one we believe in. Familiarity should not undercut the astonishing. God who entered humanity through a teenage virgin. God who was born in a manger. God who resurrected and then first appeared to *women*.[9] God who chose the most unlikely people, like fishermen and tax collectors, to be his disciples. And God who conquered the world through death.

OUR SECOND CONFESSION

All the historical, theological, and archaeological information in this book is helpful, but I know that no amount of research or facts can ever lead someone to make the second confession. Don't get me wrong. I would be remiss to omit all this information, and so much more could have been inserted—there are many hardcore theology and academic books that do just that. But I know that all the research in the world is not enough to persuade someone to wholeheartedly accept the Bible as God's Word. There is much proof that the Scriptures are God's Word, but to believe this truth only happens when information and proof are metabolized into faith.

We should remind ourselves that Christians don't know *everything* about Jesus, and yet we believe that he is the Christ. In fact, there is so much about him that we don't know. Among the myriad examples we can cite, two are that we don't know the name that is written on him (Revelation 19:12) nor the time or hour that he will return (Matthew 24:36). But we know enough. We know he is Savior, Redeemer, and the God who became man and then resurrected because he loves us. What we don't know, or will yet come to know, doesn't negate what we already know and believe about Jesus.

What we know about God is *sufficient*. God has given us enough knowledge to discern truth and believe in him.

We cannot know God fully on this earth, nor would we want to worship a god that is fully explainable and knowable with our finite human minds. The ever-expansive universe, the power of the sun, and the depth of the oceans still boggle our minds. If we have yet to understand these phenomena, how can we possibly know their Creator in full?

The same is true for the Bible. We will never know the Word of God fully on this side of eternity. We should never cease to study it, meditate on it, and obey it. And we should learn about the historical, archaeological, and theological correlations. But we will never know the Bible like we can know a literary work—the Bible can never be mastered like other books. The Word of God is immutable but is also living and active. Heaven and earth will pass away, but his words will never pass away (Hebrews 4:12, Matthew 24:35).

My deepest prayer is that this book will provide some of the proof that the Holy Spirit will transform into faith. I hope that this book has piqued your interest and whet your appetite for more studies about the Scriptures. Mostly, though, I hope everyone who reads this book professes the Scriptures to be nothing other than God's living Word, and that they turn to the Bible over and over again throughout their lives and find that it is their manna, rock, and light.

The inspired Word of God is like nothing else on the planet. Jesus used the words of Scripture to fight the devil, find courage, rebuke the haters, correct the gaslighters, and inspire the masses. He demonstrated through his life that man does not live by bread alone but by every word that proceeds out of the mouth of God (Matthew 4:4, Deuteronomy 8:3). If Jesus depended so wholly on Scripture, there is no way that we can live meaningful lives without it.

The world can seem disorienting at times because the pain can be so great. Illness, terrorism, rape, financial ruin, child abuse. When we see this kind of destruction descend on humanity, it breaks our hearts—and it can break our faith. God's Word speaks directly into such brokenness and states that this world is a fallen, sin-sick place. But it is also a beautiful place with so much hope and light.

Let us not faint or lose heart as we hold fast to the Scriptures and build on rock, one day at a time. May our lives be marked with his hesed love as we fix our eyes on Jesus, the light of the world and the light of the Word.

QUESTIONS TO PONDER

1. Have you made your second confession? Have you come to truly believe that the Scriptures are God's Word?

2. If you have yet to make the second confession, what might be the main hurdle? What is keeping you from believing that the Bible is actually God's Word?

Acknowledgments

GOD'S LIGHT CAME in the form of many people throughout the writing of this book, and I wish I had the space here to acknowledge everyone by name. Since this is not possible, I'd like to say a sincere and heartfelt thank you to all those who have been a part of this journey with me. Your timely words, insights, and encouragement have meant more to me than you can imagine. One of the brightest lights in my life has been my church family at Mariners, especially my Life Group, led by the amazing Hudys. And alongside are my former colleagues at Biola. Both are places where God's glorious light shines near and far because of the faithful leadership and servants there.

Before a single word was written, there were those who stoked the dreams of this book with prayers and encouragement. And these have been perpetual lights in my life beyond the scope of this book. Soo Jin Lee, Grace Kim, and Jessie Chung are high on this list. And my family and family-in-law top this list as only family can. I am especially grateful to my brother, Henry, whose spiritual and legal counsel made all the difference.

These people stand out front and center when I think of those who helped with the heavy lifting in writing this book: Al Hsu has been more than I could have asked for in an editor. His uncanny ability to offer the *perfect* suggestion in adding or deleting words or thoughts has made this book a million times better. He is brilliant and compassionate; when I grow up, I want to be like Al (although we're about the same age). Karen Cartmell's wise counsel and loving guidance have been used by God to heal deep parts of my soul, and her own scholarship and love for words continue to inspire me endlessly. Karen beautifully and humbly demonstrates what the Scriptures look like in faithful living. I love you dearly, Karen. Kaye and Eric Geiger's encouragement has been pivotal in the writing of this book. Eric's vast theological knowledge, shared both from the pulpit and in our conversations, has enriched my soul and mind; and Kaye's love for Jesus and his people is truly unparalleled. These incredible people are truly lights in my life and in this world.

My deepest and most profound thank you is reserved for Josephine and JD. They listened to me read *long* portions of this draft and offered invaluable insights. They told me honestly when parts were boring or too longwinded. And they cheered me on and clapped enthusiastically when they liked certain parts. They prayed for me often, even laying hands on me when I felt discouraged, uttering angelic words that can only come out of the mouths of children. They picked up extra chores, cooked me meals, took care of their own schoolwork expertly, and even offered a great reference (Herodotus!). Josephine, you truly are a fearless trailblazer with a heart of gold. This world needs leaders like you, and I know that you will be a torchbearer and culture-maker for your generation. JD, everyone who knows you loves you because they see God's light in you. You are truly a righteous young man, and your love for words, the Word, and God's people will indelibly mark this world.

Last, this book is dedicated to Brian—Light Bearer. When we were in Israel, God gave you a new name, and it's perfect. You truly are a light bearer in this dark world. And because of you, hope and healing abound. You are brilliant, humble, sacrificial, and wise. And you embody what it looks like to live out the second confession. You have made immeasurable sacrifices so that I can pursue this dream of writing, and you continue to shout and whisper words of grace and inspiration into my soul. I love you with all my heart, my husband, hero, and light bearer.

Notes

1. THE SCRIPTURES AND SALVATION

[1]I understand that *inerrant* can be a loaded term. I am not wading into the inerrancy debate here since many other disciplines, including the sciences, are intermixed. Instead I'm using this term to mean that the Bible is the inspired and true Word of God. This term also implies that "the Bible is without error in everything that it affirms," Norman Geisler and William Nix, *A General Introduction to the Bible, Revised and Expanded* (Chicago: Moody Press, 1986), 156. Also, refer to Paul D. Feinberg's analysis of the term *inerrancy* (and *infallibility*) and the importance of noting that God's Word, whether in its original writings or the copies that we currently have, is *authoritative*: Paul D. Feinberg, "Inerrancy and Infallibility of the Bible" in *Evangelical Dictionary of Theology*, 3rd ed., edited by Daniel J. Treier and Walter A. Elwell (Grand Rapids, MI: Baker Academic, 2017), 124-27. As a corollary, see Carl F. H. Henry, "Inspiration of the Bible" in *Evangelical Dictionary of Theology*, 3rd ed., edited by Daniel J. Treier and Walter A. Elwell (Grand Rapids, MI: Baker Academic, 2017), 127-29, where he notes the *trustworthiness* of Scripture.

[2]Martin Luther, "Career of the Reformer IV" in *Luther's Works 34*, edited by Helmut T. Lehmann and Lewis W. Spitz (Philadelphia: Fortress Press, 1960), 317.

[3]Some articles and books argue that Luther actually did not want to exclude the Book of James from the canon. For example, Martin Foord argues that Luther wanted to include James in the New Testament because he held to a "two-level understanding" of the Scriptures, with some books assigned to a "top tier" and others to a "lower tier" of New Testament books. Foord, however, subjects Luther's views to a theological critique and disagrees with this two-level approach to Scripture. For example, see Martin Foord,

"The 'Epistle of Straw': Reflections on Luther and the Epistle of James," *Themelios*, The Gospel Coalition, accessed November 13, 2022, www.thegospel coalition.org/themelios/article/the-epistle-of-straw-reflections-on-luther-and -the-epistle-of-james/.

[4] *Soteriology*, the doctrine of salvation through Jesus Christ, is a robust discipline involving many ideas. Specific terminology, historical understanding of the pre- and post-resurrected Jesus, and understanding of eschatology (end times) are a few of the many parts of this ongoing study. For further reference, see Jan G. Van der Watt and David S. du Toit, "Salvation" in *Dictionary of Jesus and the Gospels: A Compendium of Contemporary Biblical Scholarship*, 2nd ed., edited by Joel B. Green, Jeannine K. Brown, and Nicholas Perrin (Downers Grove, IL: IVP Academic, 2013), 826-32. This book only mentions soteriology to clarify that salvation is the biblical idea of redemption as stated in the Gospels. In essence, "Salvation is a free gift from God that rescues the believer from sin and its consequences, renews the believer to a holy life, and restores the believer to a right relationship with God for all eternity": Douglas C. Walker, "Salvation" in *Holman Illustrated Bible Dictionary*, edited by Chad Brand, Charles Draper, and Archie England (Nashville: Holman Reference, 2003), 1435.

[5] Paul Barnett, *Is the New Testament Reliable?* (Downers Grove, IL: IVP Academic, 2003), 19.

[6] Historical analysis of primary texts is helpful in discerning this process of canonization. See Robert A. Kugler's analysis of the Hebrew Bible, Septuagint (Greek translation of the Old Testament), the Dead Sea Scrolls, the New Testament, and writings of various rabbis and the early Christian church. Robert A. Kugler, "Canon" in *Dictionary of the Old Testament Historical Books: A Compendium of Contemporary Biblical Scholarship*, edited by Bill T. Arnold and H. G. M. Williamson (Downers Grove, IL: IVP Academic, 2005), 142-50.

[7] For a full discussion of varying canons used around the world and in various Christian traditions, see Karen R. Keen, *The Word of a Humble God: The Origins, Inspiration, and Interpretation of Scripture* (Grand Rapids, MI: Eerdmans, 2022), especially 61-79.

[8] R. P. C. Hanson, *Origen's Doctrine of Tradition* (London: SPCK, 1954), 93, 133; cf. his *Tradition in the Early Church* (London: SCM Press, 1962), 247, in F. F. Bruce, *The Canon of Scripture* (Downers Grove, IL: IVP Academic, 1988), 17-18.

[9] The term *breathed out* comes from the Greek word *Theopneustos*, which can also be translated into "God-spirated." Henry, "Inspiration of the Bible," 127.

[10]Although the ancient Jewish people did not use the word *canon*, they used other terms such as *sacred writings* and *authoritative writings*. Also, Scripture was noted as books that "defile the hands." This might seem counterintuitive since Scripture is sacred and would cleanse us rather than defile us. What was meant by this term is that anyone who touched the Scriptures needed to wash their hands *after* handling the Scriptures and *before* touching anything else. Geisler and Nix, *A General Introduction to the Bible*, 204-5.

[11]Bruce, *The Canon of Scripture*, 77-79.

[12]Claims to an ultimate truth and authority rests on the assertion that the canon has divine origins. For more on the divine qualities of the canon, see Michael J. Kruger, *Canon Revisited: Establishing the Origins and Authority of the New Testament Books* (Wheaton, IL: Crossway, 2012), especially 125-59.

[13]Scot McKnight, "The Jesus We'll Never Know," *Christianity Today*, April 9, 2010, www.christianitytoday.com/ct/2010/april/15.22.html.

[14]Kevin J. Vanhoozer, *The Drama of Doctrine: A Canonical-Linguistic Approach to Christian Theology* (Louisville, KY: Westminster John Knox, 2005), 146.

[15]Bruce, *The Canon of Scripture*.

[16]Geisler and Nix, *A General Introduction to the Bible*, 49.

2. OLD TESTAMENT TRADITION

[1]When we refer to the Hebrew Bible, there can be some confusion since there was the Masoretic Text, the Septuagint (Greek translation of the Old Testament), the Qumran scrolls, the Samaritan Pentateuch, and fragments from other sources (such as from the Cairo Genizah). The term *Masoretic Text* comes from the Masoretes, scribes who preserved, collected, and edited the Old Testament texts. Craig A. Evans and Emanuel Tov, editors, *Exploring the Origins of the Bible: Canon Formation in Historical, Literary, and Theological Perspective* (Grand Rapids, MI: Baker Academic, 2008), 16-17; also see Roger T. Beckwith, *The Old Testament Canon of the New Testament Church and its Background in Early Judaism* (Eugene, OR: Wipf & Stock, 1985), especially the chapters on the structure, order, number, and identity of the canonical OT books.

[2]The closing of the Old Testament canon has been in dispute in the past, mainly with the section called "Hagiographa." This section contains most of the disputed books in the canon. Historically, the Pentateuch was recognized as canonical in the fifth century BC; the Prophets were considered canonical in the third century BC; but the Hagiographa has been in dispute.

Beckwith argues against a late date of about AD 90, which some scholars, such as H. E. Ryle in *The Canon of the Old Testament*, have dated to the closing of the Hagiographa. Instead, Beckwith cites Jewish scholar S. Z. Leiman in asserting that the Hagiographa was considered canonical in the mid-second century BC rather than the late first century AD. The closing of the OT canon denotes a fixed set of books the first-century Jews would have inherited as the Scriptures. Beckwith, *The Old Testament Canon*, 4-7. The Septuagint, the Greek translation of the OT, adds another layer of consideration as many first-century Jews used this translation for the Scriptures. The Septuagint is discussed in chapter four. Norman L. Geisler and William E. Nix, *From God to Us: How We Got Our Bible* (Chicago: Moody Press, 2012), 102. Also, even if the term *canonical* is anachronistic in its usage for periods prior to Athanasius's letter in AD 367, it serves our purpose in stating which books were considered books of the divine revelation at the specified point in time.

[3]Andrew E. Hill and John H. Walton, *A Survey of the Old Testament*, 3rd ed. (Grand Rapids, MI: Zondervan, 2009), 57.

[4]Everett Ferguson, *Church History: The Rise and Growth of the Church in Its Cultural, Intellectual, and Political Context, Volume I: From Christ to the Pre-Reformation*, 2nd edition (Grand Rapids, MI: Zondervan, 2013), 31.

[5]Hill and Walton, *A Survey of the Old Testament*, 105. Also see Gordon D. Fee and Douglas Stuart, *How to Read the Bible Book by Book: A Guided Tour* (Grand Rapids, MI: Zondervan, 2002), 34; they date the exodus either at 1440 BC or 1260 BC. See discussion of exodus date in chapter three.

[6]Donald Ostrowski, *Who Wrote That?: Authorship Controversies from Moses to Sholokhov* (Ithaca, NY: Northern Illinois University Press, an Imprint of Cornell University Press, 2020), 14-15. There are many different scholars with varying dates for the Hebrew language. For example, some believe the Hebrew language was created sometime between the twelfth to the second century BC; see "About Hebrew," Yale University Library, accessed March 16, 2022, https://web.library.yale.edu/cataloging/hebraica/about-hebrew. Others suggest an earlier date; see Bruce K. Waltke and M. O'Connor, *An Introduction to Biblical Hebrew Syntax* (Winona Lake, IN: Eisenbrauns, 1990), 5-10, especially "Hebrew as a Semitic Language" and "History of Hebrew."

[7]John Calvin, *Commentaries on the First Book of Moses Called Genesis*, vol. 1, trans. John King (Grand Rapids, MI: Baker Books, 2003), 59. For reference to Moses'

authorship for Exodus, Leviticus, Numbers, and Deuteronomy, refer to John Calvin, *Commentaries on the Four Last Books of Moses Arranged in the Form of a Harmony*, vol. 2, trans. Charles William Bingham (Grand Rapids, MI: Baker Books, 2003), xiv.

[8]Karen Keen makes an insightful point that the Torah never claims that Moses is responsible for writing all, or even most, of the Pentateuch. Textual evidence reveals that Moses wrote select portions; the parts where he is referenced in the third person might indicate that additional authors or editors contributed Mosaic oral tradition or Hebrew written tradition into the Pentateuch. Karen R. Keen, *The Word of a Humble God: The Origins, Inspiration, and Interpretation of Scripture* (Grand Rapids, MI: Eerdmans, 2022), 16-17.

[9]See Bruce K. Waltke and M. O'Connor, *An Introduction to Biblical Hebrew Syntax*, 5-10.

[10]Hill and Walton, *A Survey of the Old Testament*, 81-82.

[11]Keen, *The Word of a Humble God*, 18.

[12]I am not incorporating Scripture to validate Scripture, but to insert Scripture as a historical document to see how Jesus and his first-century followers would have viewed the Pentateuch.

[13]Richard Elliott Friedman, *Who Wrote the Bible?* (New York: Harper & Row, 1987), 18.

[14]Hill and Walton, *A Survey of the Old Testament*, 79.

[15]The book of Ruth is found in the third division of the Hebrew Bible, as Ruth was not regarded as a prophet.

[16]The codex, a precursor to our modern-day book, had pages made of papyrus. Instead of traditional scrolls that could be cumbersome to carry and use, the codices allowed for parchment to be compiled in a book format. Codices enabled both sides of the papyrus to be used, with some exceptions (e.g., the book of Revelation, the *Orestes*, etc.). Also, codices allowed for several documents to be compiled into one book (like the four Gospels, originally written on separate scrolls). F. F. Bruce, *The Books and the Parchments*, revised ed. (London: Marshall Pickering/HarperCollins, 1991), 4. Further, the scrolls were eventually cut into "equal-sized sheets," stacked in a certain order, and then stacked "together along one edge. So, the scroll became a codex." *Holman Illustrated Bible Dictionary*, edited by Chad Brand, Charles Draper, and Archie England (Nashville: Holman Reference, 2003), 314.

[17]F. F. Bruce, *The Canon of Scripture* (Downers Grove, IL: IVP Academic, 1988), 30.

[18]"The Writings" are also known as the "Hagiographa," which means in Greek "holy writings," *Holman Illustrated Bible Dictionary*, 703.

[19]Bruce, *The Canon of Scripture*, 41.

[20]Bruce, *The Canon of Scripture*, 79, 82.

[21]Bruce, *The Canon of Scripture*, 31.

[22]It is anachronistic for Chronicles to follow Ezra-Nehemiah as the stories in the former immediately precede those in the latter (hence the Protestant Old Testament includes Chronicles, Ezra, and Nehemiah in this order). But one tenable theory for this ordering is that Chronicles was "canonized" after Ezra-Nehemiah. Bruce, *The Canon of Scripture*, 30-31.

[23]Bruce, *The Canon of Scripture*, 41-42.

[24]There is one reference by Josephus, the first-century Jewish historian, suggesting that the Hebrew Bible was composed of twenty-two books, rather than twenty-four. Josephus, "Against Apion" in *The New Complete Works of Josephus*, trans. William Whiston, commentary Paul L. Maier (Grand Rapids, MI: Kregel Publications, 1999), 939-40. In all likelihood, the contents are the same, with Ruth being subsumed under Judges, and Lamentations contained within Jeremiah. Bruce, *The Canon of Scripture*, 22.

3. A TIMELINE OF THE OLD TESTAMENT

[1]I learned after this realization that there are many ancient Near East (ANE) accounts of the flood, as well as other flood accounts worldwide. The parallels between the biblical account and Gilgamesh are especially interesting. The Bible affirms that the Israelites hailed from Mesopotamian roots. Hence, similarities in their literature should be expected. For example, both reveal a divine warning of impending doom, command to build a ship, animals entering the boat, torrential rains, birds sent after the flood subsides, and so on. But the flood accounts of Gilgamesh and the Bible differ in some stark and important respects. One is that Noah's ark had dimensions that are similar to modern-day ships, while the Babylonian ship would be an "unstable cube." The biggest difference, however, is the theological understanding of the flood. The Mesopotamian account asserts that overpopulation and "humanity's noise" caused the wrath of the gods, while the biblical account highlights God's anger and grief over humanity's wickedness. For more details, see Josh McDowell and Sean McDowell, *Evidence That Demands a Verdict: Life-Changing Truth for a Skeptical World* (Nashville: Thomas Nelson, 2017), 389-95. Also referenced is Andrew E. Hill and John H. Walton, *A Survey of the Old Testament*, 3rd ed. (Grand Rapids, MI: Zondervan, 2009), 80-81.

[2]The Old-Earth Creationism (OEC) theory asserts that the universe is ancient and chronologically comports with current scientific findings. The Young-Earth Creationism (YEC) theory states that the "days" of Genesis 1 are literal 24-hour days and that the whole universe, including earth, is much younger than modern science claims. Within each view are also sub-interpretations: The OEC also contains the Gap View, Day-Age View, Intermittent Day View, and Days of Divine Fiat View; and the YEC contains the 24-Hour View (within this view are three additional subcategories that harmonize with geological records, distant starlight, and dating techniques) and Mature Creation View. See McDowell and McDowell, *Evidence that Demands a Verdict*, 408-13.

[3]For example, Irenaeus in the second century believed in a "Epoch Day View," which asserts that the creation account could have lasted a thousand-year period. Others, such as Augustine in the fourth century, believed that the days of creation were not a typical calendar day. This view came to be known as the "Allegorical/Figurative Day View." McDowell and McDowell, *Evidence that Demands a Verdict*, 406-7.

[4]This statement was taken from the Latin: *In necessariis unitas, in dubiis libertas, in omnibus caritas*. Some attribute this statement to Saint Augustine, but there is no proof to this claim. Others believe that the origin stems from the seventeenth century, from Roman Catholics or Lutherans in Germany. Regardless, it is a good maxim to hold as we study the Scriptures.

[5]McDowell and McDowell, *Evidence that Demands a Verdict*, 438-39.

[6]Hill and Walton, *A Survey of the Old Testament*, 35.

[7]Hill and Walton, *A Survey of the Old Testament*, 82.

[8]Terence D. Fretheim, "Book of Exodus" in *Dictionary of the Old Testament Pentateuch: A Compendium of Contemporary Biblical Scholarship* (Downers Grove, IL: InterVarsity Press, 2003), 252. Some sources date Abraham's journey to Canaan c. 2092 BC, and the exodus from Egypt to c. 1447 BC; *Holman Illustrated Bible Dictionary*, edited by Chad Brand, Charles Draper, and Archie England (Nashville: Holman Reference, 2003), 844-45. Fretheim also notes that an earlier date (c. 1479–1425 BC) is possible, especially if the Israelites left Egypt at different times over a couple of centuries. This assertion, of course, would mean that *the* exodus event where Moses parted the sea was a different type of exodus with a mass number of Israelites leaving Egypt in close succession.

[9]Hill and Walton, *A Survey of the Old Testament*, 82.

[10]Jesus' birth is typically dated as 4 BC, but it could have been a couple of years earlier. His birth occurred during the reign of Herod the Great. Everett

Ferguson, *Church History (Volume I): From Christ to the Pre-Reformation*, 2nd ed. (Grand Rapids, MI: Zondervan, 2013), 32.

[11]Some sources contend that the Hyksos people seized control of Egypt during a time of political instability around 1730–1710 BC. They centered their power around the Nile River Delta and controlled Northern Egypt for about 250 years. The Hyksos people would have been foreign to Joseph's descendants; and the Hyksos people were eventually expelled from Egypt c. 1570 BC. *Holman Illustrated Bible Dictionary*, 844-45.

[12]Hill and Walton, *A Survey of the Old Testament*, 105. Also see Gordon D. Fee and Douglas Stuart, *How to Read the Bible Book by Book: A Guided Tour* (Grand Rapids, MI: Zondervan, 2002), 34; they date the exodus either at 1440 BC or 1260 BC.

[13]Hill and Walton, *A Survey of the Old Testament*, 105. Also see *Holman Illustrated Bible Dictionary*, 844-45.

[14]The various rules of the judges could have overlapped, which could explain the 280 years rather than the 410 total years that spanned over the lifetimes of the fifteen judges mentioned. *Holman Illustrated Bible Dictionary*, 846.

[15]*Holman Illustrated Bible Dictionary*, 848-50.

[16]The idea of the trilemma is generally attributed to C. S. Lewis, who stated: "A man who was merely a man and said the sort of things Jesus said would not be a great moral teacher. He would either be a lunatic—on a level with the man who says he is a poached egg—or else he would be the Devil of Hell. You must make your choice. Either this man was, and is, the Son of God: or else a madman or something worse." C. S. Lewis, *Mere Christianity* (New York: Simon & Schuster, 1952), 55-56. But the term *trilemma* itself has earlier roots. "Rabbi" John Duncan used this term in the middle of the nineteenth century, and Watchman Nee made a similar argument in his book *Normal Christian Faith* in 1936. See Justin Taylor, "Is C. S. Lewis's Liar-Lord-or-Lunatic Argument Unsound?," The Gospel Coalition, February 1, 2016, www.thegospelcoalition .org/blogs/justin-taylor/is-c-s-lewiss-liar-lord-or-lunatic-argument-unsound/. Also see Kyle Barton, "The History of the Liar, Lunatic, Lord Trilemma," Conversant Faith, May 4, 2012, https://conversantfaith.com/2012/05/04 /the-history-of-liar-lunatic-lord-trilemma/.

4. A CLOSE-UP OF THE OLD TESTAMENT

[1]Billy Graham, *Just as I am: The Autobiography of Billy Graham* (New York: Harper-Collins, 1997), 137-38.

[2]Graham, *Just as I Am*, 135.

[3]Graham, *Just as I Am*, 135-36.

[4]Graham, *Just as I Am*, 138.

[5]Graham, *Just as I Am*, 139.

[6]Will Graham, "The Tree Stump Prayer: When Billy Graham Overcame Doubt," Billy Graham Evangelistic Association, July 9, 2014, https://billygraham.org/story/the-tree-stump-prayer-where-billy-graham-overcame-doubt/.

[7]B. Graham, *Just as I Am*, 143-58.

[8]W. Graham, "The Tree Stump Prayer."

[9]These terms were used by the early church fathers and had the following meanings: *homologoumena* means "one word" or "in agreement"; *antilegomena* means "spoken against"; and *pseudepigrapha* means "false writings." Norman Geisler and William Nix, *A General Introduction to the Bible, Revised and Expanded* (Chicago: Moody Press, 1986), 257.

[10]Gordon D. Fee and Douglas Stuart, *How to Read the Bible Book by Book: A Guided Tour* (Grand Rapids, MI: Zondervan, 2002), 24.

[11]Fee and Stuart, *How to Read the Bible*, 34.

[12]Andrew E. Hill and John H. Walton, *A Survey of the Old Testament*, 3rd ed. (Grand Rapids, MI: Zondervan, 2009), 126-7.

[13]Hill and Walton, *A Survey of the Old Testament*, 127.

[14]Hill and Walton, *A Survey of the Old Testament*, 145.

[15]Hill and Walton, *A Survey of the Old Testament*, 145; and Fee and Stuart, *How to Read the Bible*, 49.

[16]Please refer to chapter two about Mosaic authorship of the Pentateuch, including the footnotes.

[17]Hill and Walton, *A Survey of the Old Testament*, 165-66; Fee and Stuart, *How to Read the Bible*, 55.

[18]Hill and Walton, *A Survey of the Old Testament*, 220.

[19]Hill and Walton, *A Survey of the Old Testament*, 223; Fee and Stuart, *How to Read the Bible*, 63.

[20]Hill and Walton, *A Survey of the Old Testament*, 237.

[21]Hill and Walton, *A Survey of the Old Testament*, 258.

[22]Hill and Walton, *A Survey of the Old Testament*, 282.

[23]Fee and Stuart, *How to Read the Bible*, 91.

[24]There is much controversy surrounding the authorship of Isaiah, but the consensus is that Isaiah delivered these words from God to Israel. Isaiah is considered the major source of these words, even if he did not actually write them

down himself. "We should therefore consider the eighth-century prophet Isaiah as the dominant, principle and determinative voice in the book." Hill and Walton, *A Survey of the Old Testament*, 520.

[25]Fee and Stuart, *How to Read the Bible*, 174.

[26]The MT (Masoretic Text), LXX (Septuagint), and 4QJer are the three main versions of Jeremiah that we have today. Craig A. Evans and Emmanuel Tov, editors, *Exploring the Origins of the Bible: Canon Formation in Historical, Literary, and Theological Perspective* (Grand Rapids, MI: Baker Academic, 2008), 35-36. Also, see Keen's side-by-side comparison of the MT and LXX, comparing the different arrangements of the narrative and oracles. Karen R. Keen, *The Word of a Humble God: The Origins, Inspiration, and Interpretation of Scripture* (Grand Rapids, MI: Eerdmans, 2022), 51-54.

[27]Hill and Walton, *A Survey of the Old Testament*, 534.

[28]Fee and Stuart, *How to Read the Bible*, 186.

[29]The autobiographical style of the book means there is a good probability that Ezekiel authored this book himself; there are many personal and possessive pronouns throughout. Hill and Walton, *A Survey of the Old Testament*, 555. Also, 593–571 BC are the dates of prophetic activity noted by Fee and Stuart, *How to Read the Bible*, 195.

[30]Hill and Walton, *A Survey of the Old Testament*, 582-83.

[31]Fee and Stuart, *How to Read the Bible*, 211.

[32]Hill and Walton, *A Survey of the Old Testament*, 596.

[33]Hill and Walton, *A Survey of the Old Testament*, 596-97. Fee and Stuart state the date is "uncertain" but "perhaps c. 590 BC, but possibly after 500 BC." Fee and Stuart, *How to Read the Bible*, 217.

[34]Hill and Walton, *A Survey of the Old Testament*, 607.

[35]Fee and Stuart, *How to Read the Bible*, 228; and Hill and Walton, *A Survey of the Old Testament*, 620.

[36]Either Jonah or a scribe getting information from him wrote this book. Perhaps it was someone from the "company of the prophets" (2 Kings 2:3), Hill and Walton, *A Survey of the Old Testament*, 630.

[37]Hill and Walton, *A Survey of the Old Testament*, 630.

[38]Hill and Walton, *A Survey of the Old Testament*, 642.

[39]Fee and Stuart, *How to Read the Bible*, 240.

[40]Fee and Stuart, *How to Read the Bible*, 244.

[41]Hill and Walton, *A Survey of the Old Testament*, 670.

[42]Hill and Walton, *A Survey of the Old Testament*, 678-79.

[43]Hill and Walton, *A Survey of the Old Testament*, 688-89.

[44]Fee and Stuart, *How to Read the Bible*, 262.

[45]Hill and Walton, *A Survey of the Old Testament*, 420-21.

[46]Fee and Stuart, *How to Read the Bible*, 130.

[47]Hill and Walton, *A Survey of the Old Testament*, 404.

[48]The origins of Proverbs are most likely associated with Solomon, but the full composition and redaction continued for centuries thereafter. For a full discussion of Proverbs, see Tremper Longman III, "Book of Proverbs 1" in *Dictionary of the Old Testament Wisdom, Poetry & Writings*, Tremper Longman III and Peter Enns, editors (Downers Grove, IL: IVP Academic, 2008), 539-52. Also see Hill and Walton, *A Survey of the Old Testament*, 442-43.

[49]Hill and Walton, *A Survey of the Old Testament*, 250.

[50]Fee and Stuart, *How to Read the Bible*, 78.

[51]Traditionally, this book has been dated to the late tenth century BC, both in terms of inscription and events. This date is extrapolated from verse 1:1, which credits Solomon as the author, according to traditional biblical scholarship. Due to the problems of definitive authorship, these dates cannot be accurately pinned down. Hence, a generous timeframe of "early preexilic period" is assigned to both authorship and events. Hill and Walton, *A Survey of the Old Testament*, 469-70. Also see the section "Song of Solomon" in chapter six for a fuller explanation of both the author and date of composition.

[52]Hill and Walton, *A Survey of the Old Testament*, 457-58. Also see further explanation in the section titled "Ecclesiastes" in chapter six.

[53]See further explanation in the section titled "Ecclesiastes" in chapter six.

[54]Hill and Walton, *A Survey of the Old Testament*, 544.

[55]Fee and Stuart, *How to Read the Bible*, 166. Also, the assertion that Lamentations was written soon after 586 BC makes sense since it is a part of the Megilloth and is read annually on the ninth day of Ab, which is a day of remembering and mourning the destruction of the Jerusalem temple. Hill and Walton, *A Survey of the Old Testament*, 544, 772.

[56]See the section titled "Esther" in chapter five for a fuller explanation of both the author and chronology.

[57]Daniel uses first-person narrative, which corroborates his authorship; and the places he uses the third person in the beginning chapters suggests that another person contributed to the organization and framework. See Hill and Walton, *A Survey of the Old Testament*, 568-71.

[58]Some sources state that the book was written in the second century BC (c. 165 BC); Fee and Stuart, *How to Read the Bible*, 204. Also, see a more detailed discussion regarding dates in Hill and Walton, *A Survey of the Old Testament*, 568-69.

[59]Hill and Walton, *A Survey of the Old Testament*, 331-32.

[60]Fee and Stuart, *How to Read the Bible*, 108.

[61]Hill and Walton, *A Survey of the Old Testament*, 332.

[62]Hill and Walton, *A Survey of the Old Testament*, 311-12.

[63]Fee and Stuart, *How to Read the Bible*, 99.

[64]Roger T. Beckwith, *The Old Testament Canon of the New Testament Church and its Background in Early Judaism* (Eugene, OR: Wipf & Stock, 1985), 81.

[65]Keen, *The Word of a Humble God*, 17.

[66]Beckwith notes that the Temple "was the holiest place of the nation's religious life, and the proper home for books publicly recognized as holy." Further, he notes that "not just the Law and Prophets but also the Hagiographa belonged to the Temple collection, and by the end of the Temple period had belonged to it for such a long time that it was no longer permitted even to bring in fresh copies of the books." Beckwith, *The Old Testament Canon*, 80-86; and Geisler and Nix, *A General Introduction to the Bible*, 257.

[67]B. Graham, *Just as I Am*, 135-40; W. Graham, "The Tree Stump Prayer."

[68]B. Graham, *Just as I Am*, 138.

5. READING ESTHER: A CASE STUDY

[1]The five festival scrolls in the Hebrew canon were known as the Megilloth.

[2]William W. Klein, Craig L. Blomberg, and Robert L. Hubbard, Jr., *Introduction to Biblical Interpretation* (Nashville: Thomas Nelson, 2004), 4-7. Also see E. Randolph Richards and Brandon J. O'Brien, *Misreading Scripture with Western Eyes: Removing Cultural Blinders to Better Understand the Bible* (Downers Grove, IL: InterVarsity Press, 2012).

[3]See chapter two; also see references to how perhaps earliest division was twofold (the Law and the Prophets), Norman L. Geisler and William E. Nix, *A General Introduction to the Bible, Revised and Expanded* (Chicago: Moody Press, 1986), 22, 235-55.

[4]Gordon D. Fee and Douglas Stuart, *How to Read the Bible Book by Book* (Grand Rapids, MI: Zondervan, 2002).

[5]Many sources corroborate this viewpoint that Esther is an accurate historical account during the Persian Empire. For example, Fee and Stuart note that the book of Esther shows God's "providential protection of his people during a

bleak moment in the Persian Empire," indicating that the events as told in Esther are true. Fee and Stuart, *How to Read the Bible*, 118. Also, other sources corroborate the people mentioned in the book of Esther with historical events, places, and rulers. Such examples are noted throughout this chapter; one example here is Mordecai being linked to the household of Otanes, one of the noble families of Persia. *Holman Illustrated Bible Dictionary*, edited by Chad Brand, Charles Draper, and Archie England (Nashville: Holman Reference, 2003), 510.

[6]Andrew E. Hill and John H. Walton, *A Survey of the Old Testament*, 3rd ed. (Grand Rapids, MI: Zondervan, 2009), 350-51.

[7]Hill and Walton, *A Survey of the Old Testament*, 353. Also see Fee and Stuart, *How To Read the Bible*, which states that this festival is celebrated on the fourteenth and fifteenth days of Adar, 118.

[8]Roger T. Beckwith notes that the Mishnah allows for the reading of Esther to be done in private or in public during Purim. For more on this point, see *The Old Testament Canon of the New Testament Church and its Background in Early Judaism* (Eugene, OR: Wipf & Stock, 1985), footnote 83 on page 175.

[9]Hill and Walton, *A Survey of the Old Testament*, 544, 772.

[10]Hill and Walton, *A Survey of the Old Testament*, 251.

[11]Fee and Stuart, *How to Read*, 118.

[12]F. F. Bruce's *The Canon of Scripture* (Downers Grove, IL: IVP Academic, 1988), 39; Hill and Walton, *A Survey of the Old Testament*, 350. Some other reasons that the canonicity of Esther has been debated is because it seems "unspiritual" in nature and no fragments were found among those discovered in the Qumran caves.

[13]Although the author of Esther remains anonymous, we can deduce that this person was a skillful storyteller and also had access to court records. For example, in Esther 10:2, the author mentions that Mordecai's heroics are "written in the book of the annals of the kings of Media and Persia." Further, the author clearly knows insider information and the ins and outs of the Persian court. Hill and Walton, *A Survey of the Old Testament*, 348-49.

[14]Hill and Walton, *A Survey of the Old Testament*, 349. Hill and Walton also note that the Hebrew language used in Esther shows that the book is at least older than the second century BC and probably not too much later than when the actual events took place in the fifth century BC.

[15]Even if this were true, Amestris engaged in heinous acts (such as violently mutilating Masistes, Xerxes's brother's wife) that are not consistent with the Esther of the Bible; Herodotus, *The Landmark Herodotus: The Histories*, edited by

Robert B. Strassler (New York: Anchor Books, 719). Still, it is worth noting that names in ancient sources are not always as straightforward as today. Also, Xerxes had hundreds of concubines, and to *not* be mentioned by Herodotus or other historical sources is the norm rather than the exception.

[16]Robert Gordis, "Religion, Wisdom, and History in the Book of Esther—A New Solution to an Ancient Crux," *Journal of Biblical Literature* 100, no. 3 (September 1981): 359-88. Also see John Whitcomb, *Esther: Triumph of God's Sovereignty* (Chicago: Moody Press, 1979) who shares this same opinion. Also, Marduka was known to be an "inspector," and this position as a "minor official" in the Persian court would have given him a place "in the king's gate"—a phrase attributed to Mordecai several times throughout the book of Esther.

[17]Gerald A. Larue, *Old Testament Life and Literature* (Boston: Allyn and Bacon, Inc., 1997), 363.

[18]Geisler and Nix, *A General Introduction to the Bible*, 260.

[19]E. W. Bullinger, ed., *The Companion Bible: The Authorized Version of 1611 with the Structures and Critical, Explanatory, and Suggestive Notes and with 198 Appendixes* (Grand Rapids, MI: Kregel, 1922), 85.

[20]The word *eunuch* typically refers to a male without external genitals and who was oftentimes used for royal service. *Eunuch* could also be translated in Hebrew to refer to any court official, but the eunuchs mentioned here were those who were most likely castrated (or perhaps men who were born without external genitals), especially as they were in charge of the harem or in the king's service. *Holman Illustrated Bible Dictionary*, 517.

6. DISPUTED BOOKS OF THE OLD TESTAMENT

[1]George W. Childs, *Recollections of General Grant* (Philadelphia: Collins Printing House, 1890), 40.

[2]Roger Beckwith, *The Old Testament Canon*, 321-22. "This book is included in the canon of Aquila and ranked as Scripture by Melito and Tertullian. It is also quoted, with standard formulas for citing Scripture, in the Mishnah (Taanith 4.8; Abodah Zarah 2.5)."

[3]See chapter three with timelines of the Babylonian captivity and preexilic and postexilic dates. Norman L. Geisler and William E. Nix, *A General Introduction to the Bible, Revised and Expanded* (Chicago: Moody Press, 1986).

[4]Andrew E. Hill and John H. Walton, *A Survey of the Old Testament*, 3rd ed. (Grand Rapids, MI: Zondervan, 1984), 470.

[5]Herbert Danby, trans., *The Mishnah*, Yadaim 3.5, 178-82, in Geisler and Nix, *A General Introduction to the Bible*, 259.

[6]Beckwith, *The Old Testament Canon*, 322.

[7]Hill and Walton, *A Survey of the Old Testament*, 458.

[8]Beckwith notes that Ecclesiastes has been in the canon of Josephus and the canon of Aquila; and it is also quoted in the Mishnah (Sukkah 2.6; Hagigah 1.6; Kiddushin 1.0). Beckwith, *The Old Testament Canon*, 321. Also, Ecclesiastes was used as Holy Scripture starting in the third century BC, as it was included in the Septuagint and also used by Ben Sira (c. 190–180 BC). *Holman Illustrated Bible Dictionary*, edited by Chad Brand, Charles Draper, and Archie England (Nashville: Holman Reference, 2003), 453.

[9]*Holman Illustrated Bible Dictionary*, 453.

[10]Hill and Walton, *A Survey of the Old Testament*, 457-58.

[11]Those subscribing to this traditional viewpoint are obviously very old since they predate Luther. These traditionalists believe that evidence such as Aramaic influence to date the book to a postexilic date have exaggerated this claim. They state that only seven terms are from Aramaic origins, and four of these are found in early biblical Hebrew. *Holman Illustrated Bible Dictionary*, 453.

[12]*Holman Illustrated Bible Dictionary*, 454.

[13]Billy Graham, *Words of Wisdom: A Journey Through Psalms and Proverbs* (Carol Stream, IL: Tyndale House, 2013), foreword.

[14]Edward J. Young, *An Introduction to the Old Testament* (Grand Rapids, MI: Eerdmans, 1975), 355; Geisler and Nix, *A General Introduction to the Bible*, 261.

[15]Geisler and Nix, *A General Introduction to the Bible*, 261-62.

[16]Beckwith notes the following sources as "certainly or probably" viewing Proverbs as Scripture: Ecclesiasticus, 4 Maccabees, Philo, 1 Clement, and Josephus. He also mentions the books of Romans and James in this list, and notes that Proverbs was in the canon of Aquila. Beckwith, *The Old Testament Canon*, 319.

[17]Hill and Walton, *A Survey of the Old Testament*, 442-43.

[18]Hill and Walton, *A Survey of the Old Testament*, 554-55.

[19]For example, if the details here in Ezekiel 40-48 were to be taken literally, the temple would need to be placed outside the city of Jerusalem. Young, *An Introduction to the Old Testament*, 248.

[20]Young, *An Introduction to the Old Testament*, 248.

[21]Geisler and Nix, *A General Introduction to the Bible*, 261.

[22]For example, Beckwith provides a list of proof for Ezekiel's place in the canon: "The evidence in favour of the canonicity of Ezekiel is so ample and so early

that the book is something of an embarrassment to those who hold the common view about the date of the closing of the canon. Ezekiel certainly claims to be by a divinely-commissioned prophet, and . . . the book is probably or certainly acknowledged as prophetic, biblical or divine by Tobit, Ecclesiasticus, 4 Maccabees, the Dead Sea Scrolls, the Revelation of John, 1 Clement and Josephus. . . . There is also possible attestation from Philo and from Jesus in the Gospel of John." Beckwith, *The Old Testament Canon*, 318.

[23]Beckwith, *The Old Testament Canon*, 318.

[24]E. Randolph Richards and Brandon J. O'Brien, *Misreading Scripture with Western Eyes: Removing Cultural Blinders to Better Understand the Bible* (Downers Grove, IL: InterVarsity Press, 2012), 174.

7. THE OLD TESTAMENT FAKES

[1]There are books out there that claim that Jesus was indeed married, and many try to argue that Jesus was married to Mary Magdalene. While many of these books are interesting, I don't think they persuasively prove that Jesus was married. In fact, there is no factual evidence, and many of their arguments are based on conjecture and falsified theories. Mostly, I believe that if Jesus had married someone, the Gospels would have stated so, and they don't.

[2]The historical fluidity of the canon, both Old Testament and New, shows that the "boundaries of the canon" have never been agreed upon by the global church (including the Catholic and Eastern Orthodox traditions). For Protestants, we believe the sixty-six books stand alone as canonical; but this discernment was complicated by many factors, including but not limited to the Septuagint. Karen Keen notes that "Enforcing a single canon will not prevent interpreters from extrapolating anti-Christ theologies from it. In fact, understanding our canons for what they are—closed, yet varied—is crucial for grasping the nature of the Bible and the best ways to interpret it." See Karen R. Keen, *The Word of a Humble God: The Origins, Inspiration, and Interpretation of Scripture* (Grand Rapids, MI: Eerdmans, 2022), 61-79, especially 78. As a historian, I respect the "Bible variety" within various Christian traditions; and I also value the place of noncanonical (Protestant) books in religious traditions. But as a Protestant, I still hold to the belief that the Old and New Testaments composed of sixty-six books comprise the Word of God.

[3]One that I found to be especially helpful was written by Edmon L. Gallagher and John D. Meade, *The Biblical Canon Lists from Early Christianity* (New York: Oxford University Press, 2019).

[4]Geisler and Nix, *From God to Us: How We Got Our Bible* (Chicago: Moody Publishers, 2012), 117.

[5]Roger Beckwith, *The Old Testament Canon in the New Testament Church and Its Background in Early Judaism* (Eugene, OR: Wipf & Stock, 1985), 339.

[6]For example, the apocalyptic books in the Pseudepigrapha are not all of Essene origins. There is good reason to think that 2 Baruch was of "purely Pharisaic origin" and that the Assumption of Moses and the second book of 1 Enoch are a mix between Essene and Pharisaic origin. Those not of Essene origin would not have been deemed canonical by the Essenes or any group except in very "limited circles." Beckwith, *The Old Testament Canon*, 339.

[7]The *Penitence of Jannes and Jambres* is the title given to the pseudepigraphic work concerning the Egyptian magicians who faced Moses in the book of Exodus. For further reading on this topic, consider M. R. James, "A Fragment of the 'Penitence of Jannes and Jambres,'" *The Journal of Theological Studies* 2, no. 8 (July 1901): 572-7; A. Pietersma and R. T. Lutz, "Jannes and Jambres (First to Third Centuries AD): A New Translation and Introduction" in *The Old Testament Pseudepigrapha*, ed. James H. Charlesworth (Peabody, MA: Hendrickson Academic, 2010), 427-42.

[8]Geisler and Nix, *From God to Us*, 116.

[9]Robert H. Gundry, *A Survey of the New Testament*, 5th ed. (Grand Rapids, MI: Zondervan, 2012), 24.

[10]The intertestamental period is officially known to begin after the final prophet, Malachi (c. 450 BC), is mentioned and before the birth of Christ (c. 4 BC). This period can be broken up into three main sections: The Greek Period (323–167 BC); the Period of Independence (167–63 BC); and the Roman Period (63 BC through the New Testament times). *Holman Illustrated Bible Dictionary*, edited by Chad Brand, Charles Draper, and Archie England (Nashville: Holman Reference, 2003), 829.

[11]Gundry, *A Survey of the New Testament*, 24.

[12]Alexander the Great was a mere thirty-three years old when he died in 323 BC, leaving his empire to be divided among his four generals. One quarter was taken by Ptolemy, and the Ptolemaic Kingdom of Egypt established Alexandria as their capital. The city of Alexandria was the most important Jewish settlement during the intertestamental period. Many Jews settled in this important

seaport town that facilitated much commerce and intellectual flourishing. The Jews in Alexandria eventually spoke Greek only and held onto their religion by translating the Hebrew Scriptures into Greek.

[13]Karen Keen notes that the Torah was translated into Greek "as a single project in Alexandria, Egypt, around the third century BCE," and the remaining books "of the Hebrew Bible were translated over the next century or so by anonymous scribes in unknown locations." Keen, *The Word of a Humble God*, 45. Also see Andrew E. Hill and John H. Walton, *A Survey of the Old Testament*, 3rd edition (Grand Rapids, MI: Zondervan, 1984), 494, who note that the "Greek translation of the Hebrew Old Testament was completed about 250 BC and made necessary by the impact of Hellenism on Judaism." Although the *Septuagint* (LXX) was initially the translation of only the Law from Hebrew to Greek, the term is generally used for the "pre-Christian Greek version of the whole Old Testament," and is used as such throughout this book; F. F. Bruce, *The Canon of Scripture* (Downers Grove, IL: IVP Academic, 1988), 45.

[14]These books that are in the Septuagint but not in the Hebrew Bible are sometimes called the "Septuagintal plus" and have been more commonly called the "Apocrypha" since Jerome's time. Jerome (AD 347–420) was the church father commissioned by Pope Damascus I to translate the Bible into Latin. This work became known as the Vulgate. Bruce, *The Canon of Scripture*, 48, 98-99.

[15]"Initially, the books of the Apocrypha were added one by one to *later* editions of the Septuagint [emphasis mine]. . . . These books were distinctly separated from the Hebrew Scriptures and not regarded by the Hebrews as part of the Old Testament. However, the Jewish scribes made no notation to this fact, which led to some confusion among the Greek-speaking Christians who adopted the Septuagint as their Bible." Hill and Walton, *A Survey of the Old Testament*, 494. Karen Keen notes that these deuterocanonical books were written around the "third century BCE to the first century CE." The period when the deuterocanonical books were written as noted by Keen is important. See Keen, *The Word of a Humble God*, 67-70. Finally, F. F. Bruce notes that "It was Christian writers who extended their work to the rest of the Old Testament and . . . extended that also to cover the whole of the Greek Old Testament, including those books that never formed part of the Hebrew Bible." Bruce also notes that "the Septuagint manuscripts now in existence were produced by Christians" with "few and fragmentary exceptions." Bruce, *The Canon of Scripture*, 44-45.

[16]Gallagher and Meade, *The Biblical Canon Lists*, xii. Also see Keen's "snapshot of differences" between the canons within the following traditions: Catholic,

Eastern Orthodox, Oriental Orthodox, and Protestant; Keen, *The Word of a Humble God*, 70.

[17]Gallagher and Meade, *The Biblical Canon Lists*, table of contents.

[18]Bruce, *The Canon of Scripture*, 43, and see footnote 13.

[19]For a full list of the Old Testament Apocrypha according to the Revised Standard Version and The New American Bible, see Norman Geisler and William Nix, *A General Introduction to the Bible, Revised and Expanded* (Chicago: Moody Press, 1986), 266.

[20]Tractate Sanhedrin, trans. Michael L. Rodkinson, *Babylonian Talmud*, VII-VIII, 24 found in fn. 32 in Geisler and Nix, *A General Introduction to the Bible*, 271. Also for dates see Hill and Walton, *A Survey of the Old Testament*, 703.

[21]Geisler and Nix, *A General Introduction to the Bible*, 264-66.

[22]Charles Templeton, *Farewell to God: My Reasons for Rejecting the Christian Faith* (Toronto: McClelland & Stewart, 1996), 1.

[23]Billy Graham, *Just as I Am: The Autobiography of Billy Graham* (New York: Harper-Collins, 1997), 135, 138.

[24]Templeton, *Farewell to God*, 7-8.

[25]Lee Strobel, *The Case for Faith: A Journalist Investigates the Toughest Objections to Christianity* (Grand Rapids, MI: Zondervan, 2021), 13-14, ebook.

8. MIRACLES

[1]C. S. Lewis, *Surprised by Joy: The Shape of My Early Life* (New York: HarperCollins, 1955), 272.

[2]Lewis, *Surprised by Joy*, 264.

[3]Lewis, *Surprised by Joy*, 277.

[4]Craig S. Keener, *Miracles Today: The Supernatural Work of God in the Modern World* (Grand Rapids, MI: Baker Academic, 2021), 3.

[5]Craig S. Keener, *Miracles: The Credibility of the New Testament Accounts*, volumes 1 and 2 (Grand Rapids, MI: Baker Academic, 2011), 264-358.

[6]Keener, *Miracles*, 106.

[7]Keener, *Miracles Today*, xi-xvi.

[8]Keener, *Miracles Today*, 8.

[9]Keener, *Miracles Today*, 8-9.

[10]C. S. Lewis, *Reflections on the Psalms* in *The Inspirational Writings of C. S. Lewis* (New York: Inspirational Press, 1986), 187.

[11]C. S. Lewis, *Miracles* in *The Complete C. S. Lewis Signature Classics* (New York: HarperOne, 1947), 305.

[12]Abigail Santamaria, *Joy: Poet, Seeker, and the Woman Who Captivated C. S. Lewis* (New York: Society for Promoting Christian Knowledge, 2016), 182-83.

[13]Santamaria, *Joy*, 183.

[14]Philip Yancey, "Jesus, the Reluctant Miracle Worker," *Christianity Today*, May 19, 1997, www.christianitytoday.com/ct/1997/may19/7t6080.html.

[15]In Romans 3:2 (ESV), the apostle Paul wrote, "To begin with, the Jews were entrusted with the oracles of God."

[16]Lewis, *Reflections on the Psalms*, 189.

[17]Lewis, *Reflections on the Psalms*, 189.

[18]Lewis, *Reflections on the Psalms*, 189.

[19]Lewis, *Reflections on the Psalms*, 188.

[20]Lewis, *Reflections on the Psalms*, 188.

9. A CLOSE-UP OF THE NEW TESTAMENT

[1]F. F. Bruce, *The Canon of Scripture* (Downers Grove, IL: IVP Academic, 1988), 19.

[2]The Abrahamic covenant appears in Genesis 12, where God called Abraham to leave his home in Ur and journey to Canaan. God promised to make a great nation from Abraham's seed (Genesis 12:1-3), ratified the covenant in Genesis 15, and then issued the circumcision as the external sign for the Abrahamic covenant (Genesis 17:9-14). Then, God issued the Mosaic covenant on Mount Sinai (Exodus 19), which promised David that one of his descendants would reign over God's people. Details of the Davidic covenant are extrapolated mainly from 2 Chronicles 13:5, 21:7, 23:3 and 2 Samuel 23:5. There have been a variety of interpretations regarding the Davidic covenant, mostly focusing on the "conditional or unconditional nature of the divine promises." This promise centers on David and his descendants ruling over Israel forever and culminating in a Davidic messiah. See J. J. M. Roberts, "Davidic Covenant" in *Dictionary of the Old Testament Historical Books*, eds. Bill T. Arnold and H. G. M. Williamson (Downers Grove, IL: IVP Academic, 2005), 206-11.

[3]There could have been ten authors if another John, rather than the disciple whom Jesus loved, authored Revelation. Also, the number of authors can be reduced to eight if Paul is considered the author of Hebrews.

[4]Robert H. Gundry, *A Survey of the New Testament* (Grand Rapids, MI: Zondervan, 2012), 187; Paul Barnett, *Is the New Testament Reliable?* (Downers Grove, IL: IVP Academic, 2003), 19.

⁵Daniel J. Treier, "Jesus Christ" in *Evangelical Dictionary of Theology*, 3rd ed., ed. Daniel J. Treier and Walter A. Elwell (Grand Rapids, MI: Baker Academic, 2017), 442-9. Even sources that do not acknowledge Jesus' divinity still attest to the fact that Jesus is "actually one of the best documented figures in ancient history." In fact, the "Historical Jesus" research has tried to prove that Jesus was a political revolutionary, magician, Galilean charismatic, an Essene, and eschatological prophet, among others! See John Dominic Crossan, *The Historical Jesus: The Life of a Mediterranean Jewish Peasant* (New York: Harper San Francisco, 1991), xxvii-xxviii and backflap.

⁶Barnett, *Is the New Testament Reliable?*, 23.

⁷Barnett, *Is the New Testament Reliable?*, 25-26.

⁸Barnett, *Is the New Testament Reliable?*, 28, 31.

⁹Barnett, *Is the New Testament Reliable?*, 14; see also Tacitus, *Annals of Imperial Rome*, translated by Alfred John Church and William Jackson Brodribb (Las Vegas, NV: Pantianos Classics, 2022; translation first published in 1876), 231 [ref. 15.44 in Tacitus's original publication].

¹⁰Simeon bar Kosiba was also known as Bar Kokhba with a few different forms of spelling (e.g., Kochba, Koziba, Kosba); Gundry, *A Survey of the New Testament*, 36; and *Encyclopaedia Britannica Online*, s.v., "Bar Kokhba Revolt," accessed January 24, 2023, www.britannica.com/event/Bar-Kokhba-Revolt.

¹¹Barnett, *Is the New Testament Reliable?*, 16.

¹²For a good and quick categorization into each subset, see Merrill C. Tenney, *New Testament Survey* (Grand Rapids, MI: Eerdmans Publishing Co., 1961), 125-29.

¹³Some people believe the author remains anonymous. Papias (c. AD 125), as well as some church fathers, believed that Matthew was the author, but authorship is not considered unanimous. Gordon D. Fee and Douglas Stuart, *How to Read the Bible Book by Book: A Guided Tour* (Grand Rapids, MI: Zondervan, 2002), 269. There is much proof, however, that this Gospel account was written by Matthew. Although strictly speaking all four gospels are "anonymous," uniform testimony from the early church notes that Matthew was indeed the author. Also, he would have been an "unlikely" candidate to write a Gospel account if this were a fictious work. As a former tax collector, he would have been "the most infamous character next to Judas Iscariot." For this Gospel as well as the three others, there is "uniform testimony" from the early church that affirms the authorships of Matthew, Mark, Luke, and John to the four

gospels respectively. From Lee Strobel's interview with Craig Blomberg in Strobel, *The Case for Christ*, 23.

[14]Gundry, *A Survey of the New Testament*, 189.

[15]Gundry, *A Survey of the New Testament*, 150-52.

[16]Gundry, *A Survey of the New Testament*, 152, 240. Some sources date the inscription of Luke to c. AD 70 (the fall of Jerusalem), but there is no real proof for this later date. See Fee and Stuart, *How to Read the Bible*, 286.

[17]Gundry, *A Survey of the New Testament*, 286.

[18]Gundry, *A Survey of the New Testament*, 334.

[19]Fee and Stuart, *How to Read the Bible*, 317.

[20]Fee and Stuart, *How to Read the Bible*, 333.

[21]Fee and Stuart, *How to Read the Bible*, 340.

[22]Fee and Stuart, *How to Read the Bible*, 347.

[23]Fee and Stuart, *How to Read the Bible*, 353.

[24]Fee and Stuart, *How to Read the Bible*, 359.

[25]Fee and Stuart, *How to Read the Bible*, 364.

[26]Fee and Stuart, *How to Read the Bible*, 369.

[27]Fee and Stuart, *How to Read the Bible*, 373.

[28]Fee and Stuart, *How to Read the Bible*, 379.

[29]Fee and Stuart, *How to Read the Bible*, 383.

[30]Fee and Stuart, *How to Read the Bible*, 387.

[31]Fee and Stuart note that the author was a "skilled preacher" and had an "excellent command of Greek." Also see the section on "Hebrews" in chapter ten. Fee and Stuart, *How to Read the Bible*, 390.

[32]Fee and Stuart, *How to Read the Bible*, 397.

[33]Fee and Stuart, *How to Read the Bible*, 402.

[34]Fee and Stuart note that the early church and most NT scholars question the authorship of Peter; and there is a possibility that a disciple wrote a "testament of Peter" instead. The date of composition would be around AD 64 if it was penned by Peter and later if by a disciple. Fee and Stuart, *How to Read the Bible*, 407. Also, see section titled "2 Peter" in chapter ten for a fuller explanation of both author and chronology.

[35]Fee and Stuart, *How to Read the Bible*, 411.

[36]Fee and Stuart, *How to Read the Bible*, 420.

[37]The dating seems to be in the "first Christian century" but after AD 70, since the "apostolic 'faith' seems to be well in place"; Fee and Stuart, *How to Read the Bible*, 423.

[38]Fee and Stuart, *How to Read the Bible*, 426. The author is traditionally noted as the apostle John and "son of Zebedee"; the date of composition is before the first century, although Irenaeus dated this closer to AD 180.

[39]Sometimes Philemon, 1 Peter, and 1 John are included alongside the seven disputed books, although these three are more accurately labeled "omitted" books. This means that they have been omitted from various canonical lists, rather than retained and debated among church fathers as to their canonicity.

10. INS AND OUTS OF THE NEW TESTAMENT

[1]This concept and many other vital parts of prayer are covered by this professor (alongside his coauthor, Coe) in Kyle Strobel and John Coe, *Where Prayer Becomes Real* (Grand Rapids, MI: Baker Books, 2021).

[2]There continues to be a variety of criteria for New Testament canonicity, such as good moral teaching and agreement with oral tradition. But there have been writings that were deemed both morally beneficial and a continuation of oral teachings that failed to receive canonical status. Apostolicity remains the most important criterion for New Testament canonicity. For more details, see Norman Geisler and William Nix, *A General Introduction to the Bible* (Chicago: Moody Press, 1986), 277, 283-286; Robert H. Gundry, *A Survey of the New Testament* (Grand Rapids, MI: Zondervan, 2012), 104.

[3]Gundry, *A Survey of the New Testament*, 104.

[4]The criterion of orthodoxy analyzed whether the teaching was consistent with the orthodox church—the consistent teachings about "the person and work of Christ" were critical. Catholicity measured how widely the given book was circulated in the early church. Other considerations included traditional use and matters of inspiration. See F. F. Bruce, *The Canon of Scripture* (Downers Grove, IL: IVP Academic, 1988), 256-69.

[5]Craig A. Evans and Emanuel Tov, eds., *Exploring the Origins of the Bible: Canon Formation in Historical, Literary, and Theological Perspective* (Grand Rapids, MI: Baker Academic, 2008), 26. *1 Clement* is dated in the mid-90s with "a strong possibility of the *Didache* being even earlier" (Bray, 74). The *Didache*, known as "Teaching" or "Teaching of the Twelve Apostles," was a church handbook whose date, however, has been "less certainly" cited than *1 Clement* (Beckwith, 22). Some sources, for example, date the *Didache* sometime in the late first century or between AD 100 to 110 (*Holman*, 88). Also, Bray well notes: "The core of the modern corpus [of the Apostolic Fathers] focuses on *1 Clement*, the correspondence of Ignatius, and the epistle of Polycarp. Patristic writers also recurrently

used or praised the *Epistle of Barnabas*, the *Shepherd of Hermas*, and the *Didache...*" The lack of apostolic authority precluded these well-regarded writings from canonization. Roger T. Beckwith, *The Old Testament Canon of the New Testament Church and its Background in Early Judaism* (Eugene: Wipf & Stock, 1985), 22; *Holman Illustrated Bible Dictionary*, edited by Chad Brand, Charles Draper, and Archie England (Nashville: Holman Reference, 2003), 88; Gerald Bray, "Apostolic Fathers," in *Evangelical Dictionary of Theology*, Third Edition, eds. Daniel J. Treier and Walter A. Elwell (Grand Rapids, MI: Baker Academic, 2017), 74-75.

[6]Geisler and Nix, *A General Introduction to the Bible*, 212-13.

[7]N. T. Wright, *The New Testament and the People of God: Christian Origins and the Question of God*, volume I (Minneapolis: Fortress Press, 1992), 217.

[8]Even in a highly oral and largely-nonliterate culture, followers of Christ would naturally have gravitated toward a written text for a variety of reasons, including the importance placed on covenantal texts. The Jewish people of the first century wholeheartedly believed that God commanded Moses to *write down* the law. See Michael J. Kruger, *The Question of Canon: Challenging the Status Quo in the New Testament Debate* (Downers Grove, IL: IVP Academic, 2013), 70.

[9]Geisler and Nix, *A General Introduction to the Bible*, 298.

[10]Although the author is anonymous, he most likely penned this book between AD 50–90 (most likely before AD 70 since there is no mention of the destruction of the Jewish temple).

[11]Geisler and Nix, *A General Introduction to the Bible*, 299.

[12]There is evidence that the letter was composed earlier rather than later in the first century. Gordon D. Fee and Douglas Stuart, *How to Read the Bible Book by Book: A Guided Tour* (Grand Rapids, MI: Zondervan, 2002), 397.

[13]Martin Luther, *Luther's Works: Career of the Reformer IV*, ed. Lewis W. Spitz (Philadelphia: Fortress Press, 1960), 317.

[14]John Calvin, "Acts of the Council of Trent with the Antidote," accessed November 1, 2022, www.monergism.com/thethreshold/sdg/calvin_trentantidote .html.

[15]Geisler and Nix, *A General Introduction to the Bible*, 299.

[16]Geisler and Nix, *A General Introduction to the Bible*, 299, see footnote 2 that references Everett F. Harrison *Introduction to the New Testament* (Grand Rapids, MI: Eerdmans, 1964), 345; and Donald Guthrie, *New Testament Introduction: Hebrews to Revelation* (Downers Grove, IL: InterVarsity Press, 1966), 11-18.

[17]Geisler and Nix, *A General Introduction to the Bible*, 300.

[18]Geisler and Nix, *A General Introduction to the Bible*, 300.

[19]Harrison, *Introduction to the New Testament*, 40; from Geisler and Nix, *A General Introduction to the Bible*, 300.

[20]Geisler and Nix, *A General Introduction to the Bible*, 300.

[21]Geisler and Nix, *A General Introduction to the Bible*, 300-301.

[22]Geisler and Nix, *A General Introduction to the Bible*, 301.

[23]Geisler and Nix, *A General Introduction to the Bible*, 315. This argument can be made on the premise that this work was mostly used for homiletical usage (meaning for preaching) in specific locations rather than thought to be canonical and useful for the church at large.

[24]It is preserved completely in the Codex Sinaiticus (c. AD 340), where it is found at the end of the New Testament, and also included in the table of contents of Codex Bezae (c. AD 450 or 550); *The Complete 54-Book Apocrypha*, 2022 Edition, Literal Standard Version, 626; and Geisler and Nix, *A General Introduction to the Bible*, 313.

[25]F. F. Bruce notes that this writing was perhaps the work of an Alexandrian Christian; Hippolytus of Rome (c. AD 170–235), who was considered the "last significant figure in the Roman church to write in Greek," quoted on occasion from the *Letter of Barnabas* (and *Shepherd of Hermas* and the *Didache*), but did not treat them as Scripture. Bruce, *The Canon of Scripture*, 122, 177-78.

[26]*The Complete 54-Book* Apocrypha, 626; and Geisler and Nix, *A General Introduction to the Bible*, 313.

[27]Many helpful books on the New Testament Apocrypha and Pseudepigrapha are listed at the end of this book for reference. One is Geisler and Nix, *A General Introduction to the Bible*, especially the chapter titled "The New Testament Apocrypha and Pseudepigrapha" (297-317), from which much of this information is taken.

[28]Jerome, "Epist. 120 to Hedibia and Commentary on Matthew" in Geisler and Nix, *A General Introduction to the Bible*, 306.

[29]Hennecke and Schneemelcher, "The Apocryphal New Testament," 2:276; 1:277, in Geisler and Nix, *A General Introduction to the Bible*, 306.

[30]Hennecke and Schneemelcher 1:313, in Geisler and Nix, *A General Introduction to the Bible*, 307.

[31]Hennecke and Schneemelcher 1:190, in Geisler and Nix, *A General Introduction to the Bible*, 307.

[32]Geisler and Nix, *A General Introduction to the Bible*, 313-16.

[33]Geisler and Nix, 308-12; and see Hennecke and Schneemelcher, *The Apocryphal New Testament*.

[34]Hennecke and Schneemelcher, *The Apocryphal New Testament* 1:322 in Geisler and Nix, *A General Introduction to the Bible*, 308.

11. COMPILING THE NEW TESTAMENT

[1]Olson also looks at "an old saying that 'heresy is the mother of orthodoxy' . . . In other words, what we call orthodoxy, correct Christian belief, arose largely in response to the challenges of heresies." He does qualify that "There is truth in that, and yet one has to be careful with the saying and the idea it expresses." See Roger Olson, *Counterfeit Christianity: The Persistence of Errors in the Church* (Nashville: Abingdon Press, 2015), 3, 21-22.

[2]*Holman Illustrated Bible Dictionary*, edited by Chad Brand, Charles Draper, and Archie England (Nashville: Holman Reference, 2003), 657.

[3]Some principal teachers of Gnosticism are as follows: Simon Magus (considered "the father of all heresies," but there is some confusion as to whether this Simon was Simon of Acts 8 or another Simon, and there is discussion as to whether this Simon points to Samaritan influence in the Gnostic religion); Cerinthus (supposedly the apostle John opposed him in Ephesus); Saturninus (Irenaeus writes that Saturninus taught that God made angels, and seven of these angelic beings created the world and the first man. His followers also were vegetarians and renounced marriage.); Carpocrates (he also confirmed that angels made the world but also taught reincarnation and encouraged sexual immorality, which contrasted the larger Gnostic tradition of asceticism); Basilides (he believed in 365 heavens and heavenly beings, one of whom, named Archon, was the "god" of the Jews); and Valentinus (he was the most influential Gnostic teacher, and there is some indication that the *Gospel of Truth* found at Nag Hammadi is one of his sermons). Everett Ferguson, *Church History, Volume I, From Christ to the Pre-Reformation: The Rise and Growth of the Church in Its Cultural, Intellectual, and Political Context*, 2nd ed. (Grand Rapids, MI: Zondervan, 2013), 93-95.

[4]Ferguson, *Church History*, 92.

[5]*Holman Illustrated Bible Dictionary*, 657.

[6]Ferguson, *Church History*, 88-91.

[7]Ferguson, *Church History*, 86.

[8]F. F. Bruce, *The Canon of Scripture* (Downers Grove, IL: IVP Academic, 1988), 137.

[9]Bruce, *The Canon of Scripture*, 135.

[10]For example, Montanism began in either the AD 150s or 170s when Montanus, along with two women by the names of Priscilla and Maximilla, began a

prophetic movement called the "New Prophecy" (their opponents called them the "Phrygian or Kataphrygian heresy"). Their core doctrine in terms of the Trinity or Christology did not fundamentally veer from orthodox teachings, but they emphasized prophecy and other spiritual gifts as the focal point of apostolic Christianity. Encratism (derived from the Greek word *enkrateia* meaning "self-control") focused on living a very ascetic and self-controlled Christian life. Encratites believed that human reproduction was evil and that true Christians should also abstain from wine and foods that had been sacrificed to animals. Ferguson, *Church History*, 100-101.

[11]Wright notes that the "vagaries of time have denied us" substantial historical sources from AD 30–135, but historians have labored to understand this period because pivotal events affecting Christianity have occurred during this time. Although historical documents regarding the early church are scarce during this era, historians are able to gain a "clear framework" of early believers by examining their worldview through existing sources. N. T. Wright, *The New Testament and the People of God* (Minneapolis: Fortress Press, 1992), 341, 358.

[12]For example, in Acts 18:15, Gallio, a proconsul of Achaia, tells Paul: "Since it involves questions about words and names and your own law—settle the matter yourselves. I will not be a judge of such things." This means that Gallio thought the Jewish charges against Paul were "in-house fighting" since they were of the same religion. Gallio didn't want to split hairs over semantics, so "he drove them off." Other sources note the overlapping identities between Christians and Jews prior to the burning of Rome. See Ferguson, *Church History*, 63; Paul Barnett, *Is the New Testament Reliable?* (Downers Grove, IL: IVP Academic, 2003), 63-64.

[13]Mark Noll, *Turning Points: Decisive Moments in the History of Christianity* (Grand Rapids, MI: Baker Academic, 2012), 18-19. Also, prior to AD 64, Christians did have run-ins with Roman laws, but they were not systematically recognized apart from the Jews. For example, the Roman historian Suetonius notes (in *Claudius* 25.4) that Christians were disturbing Rome c. AD 49 when Emperor Claudius expelled them from the city. Ferguson, *Church History*, 63.

[14]Noll, *Turning Points*, 22. Also, Wright notes that "the trial and execution of Christians" became "a matter of regular form" by AD 155/6 when Polycarp was burned to death in Smyrna. Wright, *The New Testament and the People of God*, 347.

[15]Tacitus, *Annals of the Imperial of Rome*, 15.44, in Ferguson, *Church History*, 63.

[16]From Dio Cassius's *Epitome* 67.14, it is noted that "high-ranking" individuals in Rome observed "Jewish customs" during Domitian's reign. Although noted as Jewish, these were most likely Christians who had some political power who Domitian wanted to curb. Trajan continued policies that allowed Christians to be punished "for the name," and Hadrian reaffirmed Trajan's policies. Marcus Aurelius's reign only increased persecution for Christians. Some of this mistreatment intersected with the Parthian war and natural disasters, such as an outbreak of a deadly plague. Ferguson, *Church History*, 64-65.

[17]Noll, *Turning Points*, 15-17.

[18]Noll, *Turning Points*, 22.

[19]Noll, *Turning Points*, 27.

[20]Bruce, *The Canon of Scripture*, 134-35.

[21]Paul Barnett, *Is the New Testament Reliable?*, 19.

[22]Valentinus, a contemporary of Marcion, hailed from Alexandria. He lived in Rome for about twenty-five years (c. AD 135–160) and was purportedly a serious candidate to become the bishop of Rome. A few Valentinian treatises were found in the Nag Hammadi documents discovered in 1945 along with the other Gnostic works. Of special importance was the *Gospel of Truth*, which was considered as the Valentinian school's manifesto. This was not a rival gospel but, rather, a meditation on the actual gospel of Jesus. In the *Gospel of Truth*, there are references to "authoritative" works that could be extrapolated as a canonical list. In the list are Matthew, Luke (possibly Acts), John, the Pauline letters (except the pastoral epistles), 1 John, Hebrews, and Revelation. Bruce, *The Canon of Scripture*, 145, and Tertullian, *Against Valentinians*, 4. The Muratorian Fragment is named after an eighteenth-century theologian, Antonio Muratori. In 1740, he published a Latin list of New Testament books that he had taken from a seventh- or eighth-century codex from Bobbio in Italy. The original list is supposedly from the second century, which was most likely written in Latin but could have had Greek influence. This document includes a list of New Testament books considered authoritative in Rome, and it also includes important observations about books deemed canonical and those that were not. Bruce, *The Canon of Scripture*, 158-68.

[23]Bruce, *The Canon of Scripture*, 180.

[24]Jerome's "peevish" ways were well known by many; he was considered to be "thin-skinn[ed]" and easily irritated. In fact, when he withdrew to the desert to become a hermit, even his fellow hermits "disliked his company." Ferguson, *Church History*, 222-23.

[25]For example, Irenaeus believed that the apostle John wrote his Gospel to refute the Gnostic belief that the true God would not enter into our world. *Holman Illustrated Bible Dictionary*, 656-57. John's focus on God's incarnate Son certainly does address this Gnostic heresy, but to definitively state John's motive for writing his Gospel as such is a bit of a stretch. God certainly used human agents and motives to write Scripture, but this type of analysis is not always helpful or accurate. Also, this supposition then implies that Gnosticism had been around prior to the writing of John's Gospel, which is dated c. AD 90–95, but most scholarship dates the Gnostic movement as an early second-century movement. *Holman Illustrated Bible Dictionary*, 656.

[26]Trevin Wax, *The Thrill of Orthodoxy: Rediscovering the Adventure of Christian Faith* (Downers Grove, IL: InterVarsity Press, 2022), 3, 9, 57.

12. THE CHURCH FATHERS

[1]Wright notes that Jesus' crucifixion was "probably to be dated in AD 30." N. T. Wright, *The New Testament and the People of God* (Minneapolis: Fortress Press, 1992), 347.

[2]Bruce notes that "The New Testament was complete, or substantially complete, about AD 100, the majority of the writings being in existence twenty to forty years before this." F. F. Bruce, *The New Testament Documents: Are They Reliable?* (Grand Rapids, MI: Eerdmans, 1981), 6-7.

[3]Norman L. Geisler and William E. Nix, *A General Introduction to the Bible* (Chicago: Moody Publishers, 1986), 288-91.

[4]Geisler and Nix, *A General Introduction to the Bible*, 420.

[5]Polycarp's letter to the Philippians is called *To the Philippians* or just *Philippians*. There is also some argument that this was not a single letter but actually two letters. F. F. Bruce, *The Canon of Scripture* (Downers Grove, IL: IVP Academic, 1988), 122. Also see Michael W. Holmes, "Polycarp of Smyrna" (specifically "The Letter of Polycarp to the Philippians") in *Dictionary of the Later New Testament and Its Developments*, ed. Ralph P. Martin and Peter H. Davids (Downers Grove, IL: InterVarsity Press, 1997), 934. Sometimes the letter is referred to as "the epistle of Polycarp." See Paul Hartog, "Apostolic Fathers" in *Evangelical Dictionary of Theology*, 3rd ed., ed. Daniel J. Treier and Walter A. Elwell (Grand Rapids, MI: Baker Academic, 2017), 74.

[6]These writings are "non-canonical early Christian writings that are also distinguished from the NT Apocrypha. The exact expression is modern, and

inconsistent criteria for inclusion have been applied, so lists vary." Hartog, "Apostolic Fathers," 74.

[7]The first collection titled *Apostolic Fathers* included the works of Clement, Ignatius, Polycarp, Barnabas, and Hermas. Eventually other works such as the *Didache* and *Diognetus* were added. *Holman Illustrated Bible Dictionary*, edited by Chad Brand, Charles Draper, and Archie England (Nashville: Holman Reference, 2003), 88. A fuller list is as follows, along with dates in parenthesis, composition location, and type of literature: *Didache* (c. 100), Syria, church order; *Barnabas* (c. 97–135), possibly Alexandria, letter/treatise; *1 Clement* (c. 96), Rome, letter/treatise; *2 Clement* (c. 100–150), possibly Corinth, sermon; *Hermas* (c. 100–155), Rome, apocalypse; *Ignatius* (c. 117), Antioch of Syria, letters; *Polycarp* (c. 115–135), Smyrna, letters; *Papias* (c. 130), Hierapolis, explanations. Taken from Everett Ferguson, *Church History, Volume I, From Christ to the Pre-Reformation: The Rise and Growth of the Church in Its Cultural, Intellectual, and Political Context*, 2nd ed. (Grand Rapids, MI: Zondervan, 2013), 49.

[8]Ferguson, *Church History*, 49.

[9]Ferguson, *Church History*, 54-55.

[10]Hartog, "Apostolic Fathers," 75.

[11]Wright notes that Polycarp's martyrdom took place about AD 155/6. This was Polycarp who was the bishop of Smyrna, which is modern-day Izmir. Wright, *The New Testament and the People of God*, 347.

[12]Taken from Geisler and Nix, *A General Introduction to the Bible*, 423. In all, a majority of the New Testament books are cited.

[13]"Justin Martyr: Defender of the 'True Philosophy,'" *Christianity Today*, accessed November 1, 2022, www.christianitytoday.com/history/people/evangelists andapologists/justin-martyr.html.

[14]Ferguson, *Church History*, 71-72. There is also the *Acts of Justin*, which is not authored by Justin but an account about his trial.

[15]Geisler and Nix, *A General Introduction to the Bible*, 425.

[16]Geisler and Nix, *A General Introduction to the Bible*, 425.

[17]Ferguson, *Church History*, 81.

[18]Geisler and Nix, *A General Introduction to the Bible*, 425, 513.

[19]Geisler and Nix, *A General Introduction to the Bible*, 425-26.

[20]Geisler and Nix, *A General Introduction to the Bible*, 426.

[21]Mark A. Noll, *Turning Points: Decisive Moments in the History of Christianity* (Grand Rapids, MI: Baker Academic, 2012), 41.

[22]Geisler and Nix, *A General Introduction to the Bible*, 427.

[23]Geisler and Nix, *A General Introduction to the Bible*, 427.

[24]Brian Kolodiejchuk, M. C., ed., *Mother Teresa: Come Be My Light: The Private Writings of the Saint of Calcutta* (New York: Image/Doubleday, 2007), 1-4.

13. COMPLETING THE CANON

[1]Robert Cowley, ed., *What If?: Eminent Historians Imagine What Might Have Been* (New York: G. P. Putnam's Sons, 2001).

[2]David McCullough, "What the Fog Wrought: The Revolution's Dunkirk, August 29, 1776" in Cowley, *What If?*, 189-200.

[3]Stephen E. Ambrose, "D Day Fails: Atomic Alternatives in Europe," in Cowley, *What If?*, 341-8.

[4]William H. McNeill, "Infectious Alternatives: The Plague That Saved Jerusalem, 701 BC," in Cowley, *What If?*, 3.

[5]McNeill, "Infectious Alternatives," 5-6.

[6]McNeill, "Infectious Alternatives," 6.

[7]McNeill, "Infectious Alternatives," 9-11.

[8]McNeill, "Infectious Alternatives," 10.

[9]McNeill, "Infectious Alternatives," 10-11.

[10]Books in our NT that are not in the Muratorian Canon: 1 Peter, 2 Peter, James, and Hebrews. Mark A. Noll, *Turning Points: Decisive Moments in the History of Christianity* (Grand Rapids, MI: Baker Academic, 2012), 29.

[11]Codex Sinaiticus (c. 340–350) contains the oldest complete copy of the New Testament (with the exclusion of Mark 16:9-20 and John 7:53-8:11), over half of the LXX, and a majority of the OT Apocrypha. Codex Vaticanus (c. 325–350) is also a very important document that contains most of the LXX, most of the NT (missing are 1 Timothy through Philemon, Hebrews 9:14 to the end of the New Testament, and the General Epistles), and a majority of the OT Apocrypha. See F. F. Bruce, *The Canon of Scripture* (Downers Grove, IL: IVP Academic, 1988), 205-7; Norman Geisler and William Nix, *A General Introduction to the Bible* (Chicago: Moody Press, 1986), 388-402; Karen Keen, *The Word of a Humble God: The Origins, Inspiration, and Interpretation of Scripture* (Grand Rapids, MI: Eerdmans, 2022), 20-23. Also, Keen dates the Codex Sinaiticus at c. 350, Geisler and Nix date it at c. 340, and Bruce notes just "fourth century."

[12]Six parallel columns compared the Hebrew Old Testament, the Septuagint, a Greek transliteration, the Greek translations of Aquila, Symmachus, and Theodotion. Everett Ferguson, *Church History, Volume I, From Christ to the*

Pre-Reformation: The Rise and Growth of the Church in Its Cultural, Intellectual, and Political Context, 2nd ed. (Grand Rapids, MI: Zondervan, 2013), 132.

[13]Geisler and Nix, *A General Introduction to the Bible*, 420-1.

[14]Geisler and Nix, *A General Introduction to the Bible*, 281.

[15]Eusebius, "Ecclesiastical History 8.2," in Geisler and Nix, *A General Introduction to the Bible*, 279.

[16]Eusebius "Ecclesiastical History 8.2," 279.

[17]Noll, *Turning Points*, 40-41.

[18]Noll, *Turning Points*, 45.

[19]Noll, *Turning Points*, 42.

[20]Geisler and Nix, *A General Introduction to the Bible*, 282.

[21]Noll, *Turning Points*, 42.

[22]As emperor, Diocletian divided the vast Roman Empire into four districts. In the very west, Constantius Chlorus, Constantine's father, was installed as the head. The four districts became three in 305 when Diocletian abdicated the throne. In 312, Constantine arose as one of the final rulers when he defeated Maxentius at the Battle of Milvian Bridge. He was co-emperor with Licinius until 324, when Constantine became sole emperor.

[23]Interestingly, each of these terms shows Jesus' divinity. For example, Jesus refers to himself as the Son of Man more than any other title in the synoptic gospels. *Son of Man* wasn't highlighting Jesus' humanity, but, rather, it was referencing Daniel 7:13-14, where "one like a son of man" was given "an everlasting dominion," and "His kingdom is one that will never be destroyed."

[24]Noll, *Turning Points*, 40-45.

[25]Noll, *Turning Points*, 46-47.

[26]Noll, *Turning Points*, 48-49.

[27]Saint Athanasius, *On the Incarnation*, trans. by John Behr and preface by C. S. Lewis (Yonkers: St. Vladimir's Seminary Press), 34.

[28]A more accurate term is the *Nicaeno-Constantinopolitan Creed*.

[29]Noll, *Turning Points*, 50-51. Prior to this council of 381, of course, many trinitarian discussions and debates continued throughout the fourth century. In Acts 13:2, the "Holy Spirit said, 'Set apart for me Barnabas and Saul for the work to which I have called them." Also many other passages note the workings of the third part of the Trinity.

[30]Noll, *Turning Points*, 24.

[31]Geisler and Nix, *A General Introduction to the Bible*, 421.

[32]Noll, *Turning Points*, 29.

[33]Athanasius in Noll, *Turning Points*, 26.

14. ANSWERING CHALLENGES TO SCRIPTURE

[1]This is the oldest complete manuscript of the Hebrew Bible in Hebrew. Also, the Aleppo Codex dates a few decades before the Leningrad Codex, but it's missing a significant part of the Torah. Karen Keen, *The Word of a Humble God: The Origins, Inspiration, and Interpretation of Scripture* (Grand Rapids, MI: Eerdmans, 2022), 23. Also note that "*Codex Leningradensis* . . . [was] dated to AD 1008," in Paul D. Wegner, "The Reliability of the Old Testament Manuscripts" in *Understanding Scripture: An Overview of the Bible's Origin, Reliability, and Meaning*, ed. Wayne Gruden, C. John Collins, and Thomas R. Schreiner (Wheaton, IL: Crossway, 2012), 108.

[2]Michael F. Bird, *Seven Things I Wish Christians Knew about the Bible* (Grand Rapids, MI: Zondervan Reflective, 2021), 3.

[3]Bird notes that the Codex Vaticanus is "the oldest complete copy of the Greek New Testament," but this codex is missing some important books of the NT. Codex Vaticanus (c. AD 325–350) contains most of the LXX, most of the NT (but missing are "1 Timothy through Philemon, Hebrews 9:14 to the end of the New Testament, and the General Epistles"), and a majority of the OT Apocrypha. Codex Sinaiticus (c. 340) contains the oldest complete copy of the New Testament (with the exclusion of Mark 16:9-20 and John 7:53-8:11), over half of the LXX, and a majority of the OT Apocrypha. The John Rylands Fragment (c. AD 117–138) is the earliest known copy of any part of the NT, it "contains portions of five verses from the gospel of John (John 18:31-33, 37-38)." There are many, many other important fragments and codices: Chester Beatty Papyri (c. AD 250) which contains most of the New Testament but is missing parts of Romans and 1 Thessalonians, as well as all of 2 Thessalonians. The Bodmer Papyri (second–third century AD) includes John 1:1-6:11, 6:35b-14:26, and fragments from John 14-21. It also contains the earliest known copy of Jude, 1 Peter, and 2 Peter, and also some apocryphal books. See Bird, *Seven Things*, 18; Norman Geisler and William Nix, *A General Introduction to the Bible, Revised and Expanded* (Chicago: Moody Press, 1986), 388-402; William J. Falls, "Codex," in *Holman Illustrated Bible Dictionary*, edited by Chad Brand, Charles Draper, and Archie England (Nashville: Holman Reference, 2003), 314; Keen, *The Word of a Humble God*, 20-23; F. F. Bruce's *The Canon of Scripture* (Downers Grove: IVP Academic, 1988), 205-7.

[4] Lee Strobel, *The Case for Christ: A Journalist's Personal Investigation of the Evidence for Jesus* (Grand Rapids, MI: Zondervan, 2016), 62-63.

[5] Strobel, *The Case for Christ*, 64-67. Strobel notes that there are 5,664 Greek manuscripts cataloged as of the publication of his book.

[6] This quote comes from Sir Frederic Kenyon (author of *The Paleography of Greek Papyri*) and found in Strobel's *The Case for Christ*, 67.

[7] Strobel, *The Case for Christ*, 65-69.

[8] Bart D. Ehrman, *Misquoting Jesus: The Story Behind Who Changed the Bible and Why* (New York: HarperOne, 2005).

[9] See Robert B. Stewart, ed., *The Reliability of the New Testament: Bart D. Ehrman and Daniel B. Wallace in Dialogue* (Minneapolis: Fortress Press, 2011), especially pages 13-60.

[10] Ehrman, *Misquoting Jesus*, 51-55.

[11] Daniel B. Wallace, "Lost in Transmission: How Badly Did the Scribes Corrupt the New Testament Text?" in *Revisiting the Corruption of the New Testament: Manuscript, Patristic, and Apocryphal Evidence*, ed. Daniel B. Wallace (Grand Rapids, MI: Kregel Academic, 2011), 26-27.

[12] Daniel B. Wallace, "The Reliability of the New Testament Manuscripts" in *Understanding Scripture: An Overview of the Bible's Origin, Reliability, and Meaning*, ed. Wayne Gruden, C. John Collins, and Thomas R. Schreiner (Wheaton, IL: Crossway, 2012), 114-15.

[13] Wallace, "The Reliability of the New Testament Manuscripts," 116.

[14] Wegner, "The Reliability of the Old Testament Manuscripts," 101-7.

[15] Keen, *The Word of a Humble God*, 12.

[16] Wegner, "The Reliability of the Old Testament Manuscripts," 104-7.

[17] Jean-Pierre Isbouts, *Archaeology of the Bible: The Greatest Discoveries from Genesis to the Roman Era* (Washington, DC: National Geographic, 2016), 26-28.

[18] Strobel, *The Case for Christ*, 106-7.

[19] Strobel, *The Case for Christ*, 106, cites Norman Geisler and Thomas Howe, *When Critics Ask* (Wheaton, IL: Victor, 1992), 385.

[20] Strobel, *The Case for Christ*, 117, cites John Ankerberg and John Weldon, *The Facts on the Mormon Church* (Eugene, OR: Harvest House, 1991), 30, emphasis in original.

[21] Josh McDowell and Sean McDowell, *Evidence that Demands a Verdict: Life-Changing Truth for a Skeptical World* (Nashville: Thomas Nelson, 2017), 230.

[22] McDowell and McDowell, *Evidence that Demands a Verdict*, 230-31.

[23]Charles Colson cited by Marty Angelo, "How Chuck Colson's Legacy of Hope Lives On," Prison Fellowship, accessed May 8, 2022, www.prisonfellowship .org/2018/04/chuck-colsons-legacy-hope-lives/.

15. BUILD ON ROCK

[1]The Sermon on the Mount is in Matthew 5-7. Interestingly, this sermon is known as the "most commented upon portion of Scripture throughout the church's history." Jonathan T. Pennington, *The Sermon on the Mount and Human Flourishing: A Theological Commentary* (Grand Rapids: Baker Academic, 2017), 1-2.

[2]C. S. Lewis, *The Screwtape Letters* (New York: Simon & Schuster, 1961), 29.

[3]Words of Craig Blomberg from Lee Strobel, *The Case for Christ: A Journalist's Personal Investigation of the Evidence for Jesus* (Grand Rapids, MI: Zondervan, 2016), 45.

[4]*Holman Illustrated Bible Dictionary*, ed. Chad Brand, Charles Draper, and Archie England (Nashville: Holman Bible Publishers, 2003), 756.

[5]Michael Card, *Inexpressible: Hesed and the Mystery of God's Lovingkindness* (Downers Grove, IL: InterVarsity Press, 2018), 3-5.

[6]John Calvin, *Commentary on the Gospel According to* John, trans. William Pringle (Grand Rapids, MI: Baker Book House, 2003), 26.

[7]Andrew E. Hill and John H. Walton, *A Survey of the Old Testament*, 3rd edition (Grand Rapids, MI: Zondervan, 2009), 64. Also, see Karen R. Keen's interesting explanation on the dating of the Old and New Testaments, *The Word of a Humble God: The Origins, Inspiration, and Interpretation of Scripture* (Grand Rapids, MI: Eerdmans, 2022), 16-21.

[8]Aramaic is a Semitic language that was widely used in the ancient Near East starting from about the sixth century BC and became the common language of the Jewish people. See Bruce K. Waltke and M. O'Connor, *An Introduction to Biblical Hebrew Syntax* (Winona Lake, IN: Eisenbrauns, 1990), 12-16.

[9]In Jesus' society, women were not given much authority, and their testimonies would not have held much weight. See Strobel, *The Case for Christ*, 253-54.

Further Reading

Aharoni, Yohanan. *The Land of the Bible: A Historical Geography, Revised and Enlarged Edition*. Philadelphia: The Westminster Press, 1979.

Andrews, Edward D. *Misrepresenting Jesus: Debunking Bart D. Ehrman's 'Misquoting Jesus.'* Cambridge, OH: Christian Publishing House, 2019.

Barnett, Paul. *Is the New Testament Reliable?* Downers Grove, IL: IVP Academic, 2003.

Beckwith, Roger. *The Old Testament Canon of the New Testament Church and Its Background in Early Judaism*. Eugene, OR: Wipf and Stock, 2008.

Bird, Michael F. *Seven Things I Wish Christians Knew About the Bible*. Grand Rapids, MI: Zondervan Reflective, 2021.

Blomberg, Craig L. *Can We Still Believe the Bible?: An Evangelical Engagement with Contemporary Questions*. Grand Rapids, MI: Brazos Press, 2014.

Blomberg, Craig L. *The Historical Reliability of the Gospels*. Downers Grove, IL: InterVarsity Press, 1987.

Blomberg, Craig L. *Making Sense of the New Testament: Three Crucial Questions*. Grand Rapids, MI: Baker Academic, 2004.

Bruce, F. F. *The Books and the Parchments: Some Chapters on the Transmission of the Bible*. Rev. ed. Westwood, NJ: Fleming H. Revell Company, 1963.

Bruce, F. F. *The Canon of Scripture*. Downers Grove, IL: IVP Academic, 1988.

Bruce, F. F. *The New Testament Documents: Are They Reliable?* Grand Rapids, MI: Eerdmans, 1981.

Clements, Ronald E. *Old Testament Prophecy: From Oracles to Canon*. Louisville, KY: Westminster John Knox Press, 1996.

Collins, John J., Craig A. Evans, and Lee Martin McDonald. *Ancient Jewish and Christian Scriptures: New Developments in Canon Controversy*. Louisville, KY: Westminster John Knox Press, 2020.

Evans, Craig A. and Emanuel Tov, eds. *Exploring the Origins of the Bible: Canon Formation in Historical, Literary, and Theological Perspective*. Grand Rapids, MI: Baker Academic, 2008.

Fee, Gordon D. and Douglas Stuart. *How to Read the Bible Book by Book: A Guided Tour*. Grand Rapids, MI: Zondervan, 2002.

Fee, Gordon D. and Douglas Stuart. *How to Read the Bible for All Its Worth: A Guide to Understanding the Bible*, 2nd ed. Grand Rapids, MI: Zondervan Publishing House, 1993.

Geisler, Norman L. and William E. Nix. *A General Introduction to the Bible.* Rev. and exp. ed. Chicago, IL: Moody Press, 1986.

Geisler, Norman L. and William E. Nix. *From God to Us: How We Got our Bible.* Chicago: Moody Publishers, 2012.

Geisler, Norman L. and Frank Turek. *I Don't Have Enough Faith to Be an Atheist.* Wheaton, IL: Crossway, 2004.

Grudem, Wayne. *Bible Doctrine: Essential Teachings of the Christian Faith.* Edited by Jeff Purswell. Grand Rapids, MI: Zondervan Academic, 1999.

Grudem, Wayne, C. John Collins, and Thomas R. Schreiner, eds. *Understanding Scripture: An Overview of the Bible's Origin, Reliability, and Meaning.* Wheaton, IL: Crossway, 2012.

Guthrie, Donald. *New Testament Introduction.* Downers Grove, IL: InterVarsity Press, 1975.

Holden, Joseph M. and Norman Geisler. *The Popular Handbook of Archaeology and the Bible: Discoveries that Confirm the Reliability of Scripture.* Eugene, OR: Harvest House Publishers, 1995.

Jones, Timothy Paul. *Misquoting Truth: A Guide to the Fallacies of Bart Ehrman's Misquoting Jesus.* Downers Grove, IL: InterVarsity Press, 2007.

Keen, Karen R. *The Word of a Humble God: The Origins, Inspiration, and Interpretation of Scripture.* Grand Rapids, MI: Eerdmans, 2022.

Klein, William W., Craig L. Blomberg, and Robert L. Hubbard, Jr. *Introduction to Biblical Interpretation.* Nashville: Thomas Nelson, 2004.

Kruger, Michael J. *Canon Revisited: Establishing the Origins and Authority of the New Testament Books.* Wheaton, IL: Crossway, 2012.

Kruger, Michael J. *The Question of Canon: Challenging the Status Quo in the New Testament Debate.* Downers Grove, IL: IVP Academic, 2013.

Lewis, C. S. *Miracles* in *The Complete C. S. Lewis Signature Classics.* New York: HarperOne, 1947.

Lightfoot, Neil R. *How We Got the Bible.* Grand Rapids, MI: Baker, 2010.

Luther, Martin. *Career of the Reformer IV.* Edited by Helmut T. Lehmann and Lewis W. Spitz, Luther's Works 34. Philadelphia: Fortress Press, 1960.

McDowell, Josh and Sean McDowell. *Evidence That Demands a Verdict: Life-Changing Truth for a Skeptical World, the Completely Updated and Expanded Classic.* Nashville: Thomas Nelson, 2017.

McRay, John. *Archaeology and the New Testament.* Grand Rapids, MI: Baker Academic, 1991.

Metzger, Bruce M. *The New Testament: Its Background, Growth, and Content.* 3rd edition, revised and enlarged. Nashville: Abingdon Press, 2003.

Nelson, Richard D. *The Old Testament: Canon, History, and Literature.* Nashville: Abingdon Press, 2019.

Noll, Mark A. *Turning Points: Decisive Moments in the History of Christianity.* Grand Rapids, MI: Baker Academic, 2012.

Patzia, Arthur G. *The Making of the New Testament: Origin, Collection, Text and Canon.* Downers Grove, IL: IVP Academic, 2011.

Porter, Stanley E. *How We Got the New Testament: Text, Transmission, Translation.* Grand Rapids, MI: Baker Academic, 2013.

Reeves, Ryan M. and Charles E. Hill. *Know How We Got Our Bible.* Grand Rapids, MI: Zondervan, 2018.

Richards, E. Randolph and Brandon J. O'Brien. *Misreading Scripture with Western Eyes: Removing Cultural Blinders to Better Understand the Bible.* Downers Grove, IL: InterVarsity Press, 2012.

Steward, Robert B., ed. *The Reliability of the New Testament: Bart D. Ehrman & Daniel B. Wallace in Dialogue.* Minneapolis: Fortress Press, 2011.

Strobel, Lee. *The Case for Christ: A Journalist's Personal Investigation of the Evidence for Jesus.* Grand Rapids, MI: Zondervan, 2016.

Tenney, Merrill C. *New Testament Survey.* Grand Rapids, MI: Eerdmans, 1961.

VanderKam, James C. *The Dead Sea Scrolls Today.* Grand Rapids, MI: Eerdmans, 1994.

Vanhoozer, Kevin J. *The Drama of Doctrine: A Canonical-Linguistic Approach to Christian Theology.* Louisville, KY: Westminster John Knox, 2005.

Wallace, Daniel B., ed. *Revisiting the Corruption of the New Testament: Manuscript, Patristic, and Apocryphal Evidence.* Grand Rapids, MI: Kregel Academic, 2011.

Wegner, Paul D. *The Journey from Texts to Translations: The Origin and Development of the Bible.* Grand Rapids, MI: Baker, 1999.

Wright, N. T. *The New Testament and the People of God: Christian Origins and the Question of God.* Volume I. Minneapolis: Fortress Press, 1992.

Yamauchi, Edwin M. *The Scriptures and Archaeology: Abraham to Daniel.* Eugene, OR: Wipf & Stock, 1980.

Young, Edward J. *An Introduction to the Old Testament.* Grand Rapids, MI: Eerdmans, 1975.